# SHOCK
## and AWE

The Spiritual Journey of Coyote Chris Sutton

*Coyote*

# CHRIS SUTTON

*with Dave Nunnally*

*First Edition:*
First printing

PUBLISHED BY HAUNTED ROAD MEDIA, LLC

www.hauntedroadmedia.com

United States of America

Dad, I can just see you in the Spirit world talking to those authors whose works you love so much. When it is my time to make the journey, I will bring you a copy of this book.
I think you will like it.

# Acknowledgments

You never get anywhere in life without the help of others and I owe thanks to the following people for their help and inspiration for me to do the videos and then this book.

Mike Ricksecker and Haunted Road Media for taking me on and helping me publish this book. His quiet confidence in me helped me to keep trying until I was able to finally make this dream come through.

My spiritual brothers and sisters of the Red Cedar Circle: Johnny Moses, Kathy Sundown, Bill Coty, Greg Fields, Jay Worthy, Kathy Matthews, Deloris Elie, and Katja Kopp. E Hychka Siam!

Dave and Donna Nunnally of It's Raining Zen in Alton, IL who have been so generous with their time, space, and support that they have shared with myself and my family. Without them the videos and the book may never have happened. Love you both!

Elizabeth Saint and Vidispace for believing that a video of an interview with me would be a good fit for their streaming platform. El, your Uncle Coyote is eternally grateful.

All my friends in my paranormal world who are like another family to me. Too many to name, but I know who you all are. I will be talking more about you in the future, so stay tuned.

Jeremy Baker, whose intuitive tattoo creations brought the symbols of my spiritual path to life. You are a true artist, my friend! (Check his work out on IG at @j.baker_atc)

Jordan Bruce, whose videography and editing of the videos made such a difference. Don't go anywhere, kid, we'll have more work to do later.

Dr. Andrew Carr, my chiropractor supreme. He knows what I need to keep my body in one piece, whether I tell him where it hurts or not, for he knows the ways of The Force.

The crew from Coyote Chris' Crazy Chaotic Spiritual Circle: Lin, Carla, Kimberly, Ashley, Amanda, Rachael, Sara, Chaz, Donna, Kathy, Autumn, Aaron, and Deb. You all are the best!

My video podcast partners and friends Sharla Harden (The Spirit Drum) and Wes Forsythe (Scarefest Television). You both inspire me to do better and I think the world of you both.

Emily and Max, you have both been a delight and I could not ask for a better daughter and son. I love you both so much. You grew up with a dad who was a bit different and now you are both uniquely different in your own ways and I could not be prouder of both of you.

Julia, what a road we have walked. You went from being a non-believer to someone whose skills I trust such that we do investigations together now. Your support keeps me going and you know when to pull me out of the clouds. It has been a good 30 years and I love you more than I can say.

# Table of Contents

# Introduction

This book was born out of two video interviews I did with Dave Nunnally that were filmed in late 2018 and during the summer of 2019. Dave and I shot the first one ourselves and then we turned it over to the more capable hands of Jordan Bruce of Jordan Bruce Photography to shoot the second interview and then edit both. These videos can be seen on the streaming platform Vidispace. Now, the videos stand well on their own, but I had another itch I needed to scratch. I had been trying for years to put a book together. Now, I know people who can sit and write as easy as falling out of bed and put out beautiful prose. Not me. If each of the books I had started was a totaled-out car I could make a junkyard out of them. So, one day I was dreaming of seeing my name on a book cover when an idea hit me. What if I had the videos transcribed and then make a book out of that? I thought, "That's genius!" But then I remembered that I had fooled myself before. So, I got ahold of my friend, Mike Ricksecker, who owns Haunted Road Media and who had been so supportive of my previous book attempts, and I asked him how I could make these videos into books. Then he told me how, and I went out and did it. I got them transcribed into printed text. Sound easy? You would think, but hell no. It still took lots of editing and lots of rewriting, and screaming, "Sutton! Quit saying, 'you know!'". I have vowed to never utter these words together again during any kind of audio or video production I am involved in. But I did it, I got it done.

Dave got his part done, too. Now, if you watch the videos and read this book, you will notice early on that there are differences. That is because as I was editing the transcription, I realized that not everything that was said during the videos would translate well to the page. It was a you-had-to-be-there kind of situation. Plus, I did not know what questions Dave was going to ask, and I answered with whatever popped in my mind without a tremendous amount of thought. So, when editing and writing this book I added details to my answers to Dave's questions and cleaned up much of my word salad so that I made sense in print, and now it is a work that I can live with. All Coyote levity aside, this book reflects the path I have walked for over 25 years, and I hope that you will find something in here that motivates you to find your medicine so you can walk with Spirit and make a difference in this world.

# PART I

# SHOCK

*and*

# AWE

# Part 1

## Shock and Awe

Dave:

I don't know where to begin with Chris Sutton – he is a fascinating man, but he is also an enigma. I learn more from Chris each time I work with him and what I can share is this: he is a multi-faceted man, a great conversationalist, an insightful healer, a paranormal investigator, a shaman, a musician, and a kind and compassionate soul – Chris is many things to many people. From the moment he first experienced his awakening at a pow-wow, he has followed his path wherever it has led him, or as Chris says, "bringing light to the darkest places." Chris and his family have become family to me; he is not only my good friend, but he is also my brother I happened to meet in the second half of life. But to really understand Chris, I have to dive back into his life before Coyote Chris Sutton emerged in the Riverbend. Who is Chris Sutton?

Coyote Chris:

I've been many different people, it seems like, but I am from

Alton, Illinois, where we are recording right now, and I went to school here in this area. I went to Alton Senior High School and graduated from there and played football and wrestled and things like that. I went to college in this area first at Lewis and Clark Community College and then I ended up in Springfield, Illinois, where I graduated from Sangamon State University with a bachelor's degree in Social Justice. Who am I? I mean, that's been an evolving thing for the last, shit, I mean since I was born, of course, but I mean, it's shifted. I was just a "normal" person, like we're talking earlier, about being a high school student who was a jock and all that kind of stuff and not really having any religious background. I was raised as a Unitarian and of course they are more like humanists, secular humanists they're called, and they don't often go in for Jesus and stuff like that. It's more philosophical. And so that's how I was raised as far as religion things go but you know, there's other things. My father was an English teacher, and he loved teaching the Greek epics, Homer was a favorite of his, and he taught the Illiad and the Odyssey. So, I grew up hearing stories of Odysseus and Achilles and Hector and all these heroes from the Trojan War and things like that. But that was me, that was my religious thing right there, you know, the Greek gods and things like that. I wasn't into the gods, per se, but it was just sort of where I was at, I loved the hero aspects of these stories. I guess I lived my life just pretty much as an agnostic as I grew up, then started my career, got married, and I had one child when shit started to hit the fan.

I have two grown children now, but my story really starts after I had my first child. Gosh, how many years ago? 25? I was 35. I know that I was 35 years old. Emily was born in 1992, so it was probably 1993 when it happened. You asked about who am and this event changed my life like an earthquake changes the landscape. My landscape got shook up. It had happened to me, my own personal earthquake. So, when this happened, we lived in little town called Onarga, Illinois. It's about 45 minutes north of Champaign, which is where the University of Illinois is. It was a little bitty town, 1400 people, in a little bitty county, Iroquois, of probably about maybe 10,000 people, if that.

So, my wife, Julia, she comes to me one day and she goes, "I want to go to the pow-wow." I said, "What pow-wow are you talking about?" And she goes, "Oh, there's a pow-wow in Watseka." (Now Watseka is the seat of Iroquois County and that's the only town that had a hospital in the county and so that's where my daughter had been born.). I didn't know anything about this sort of thing. I mean, I knew about Native American history and things like that, and was always very sympathetic to the way they had been treated, because I thought they really, really, really got a raw deal as far as getting their land taken from them and the attempted genocide of their people and all that kind of stuff. But I'd never really looked at the culture as it is today, nor their spiritual traditions.

Now, Julia used to be a pow-wow dancer and so she was really interested in this. I love to tell this story because I always tell everybody how I went through my change and I always say that it's her fault. She's the one who took me to this place where it happened. And so, we go to the pow-wow, and it's not just any pow-wow, it's the freaking Pow-Wow Nationals. So, we got people from across the United States and Canada in this small rural county in Illinois. It was held at the fairgrounds, the county fairgrounds. Now, at these fairgrounds they are usually judging cows and pigs and things like that and doing whatever they do at those tractor pulls and cow patty bingo events, but this day was different. The pow-wow had a grand arena and then in the middle they have the have the judges, the announcers and other people like that. And then the drums, you know, the big drums with four guys are sitting around doing the drumming and singing. And so, we're watching that and I'm thinking that this is pretty cool because it's so amazingly colorful as all the different tribes have their own regalia. (Regalia is what the dancers wear, they are not called "costumes.") They all wear different colors and they all dance in different styles. Northern dancers dance slowly, and the southern dancers dance more quickly and so you got different drums for different dances. So, I'm taking all this stuff in and I'm thinking this is really kind of neat, and I realized this is a part of their culture.

I knew nothing about what this was really, but I wasn't awed by it all yet. I just saw it as a really interesting experience, but then I hear some drumming off in the distance, in this livestock barn. It was real strong and rhythmic and I'm like, "Okay, I'll check this out and see what's going on." I wandered away from the main arena and I walked in this barn and the drums are just, boom, boom, boom, boom and the rattles are shaking, and the dancers were chanting. I found out later it was a warrior's dance called a Gourd Dance, and veterans and sons of veterans are the only people allowed to do these dances. It was very powerful in this enclosed area, and the drumming was just throbbing through my body. Then I started to feel it, so I started to kind of shake my head to the drumming. Then all of a sudden, I went… it was like I went someplace else. Then I realized that I was not in this reality, not totally in this world anymore. I had one foot in our world, or what we would call our world, and a foot in another world, which I now define as Spirit, at the same time. It scared the crap out of me. I'm like, "What is this!" It was so profound. The Buddhist call it a satori when we get a big spiritual breakthrough, something just happens to you that just arrests your thoughts, arrests everything. And you are just totally in the moment. Nothing else meant anything to me at all at that point in time, other than to be awed, shocked and awed, by this whole experience. I'd been interested in music most of my life, but I had never been brought to a different world by music before. It woke something up in me.

I learned in shamanism later that drums are used to journey and that to journey means to leave our world. Part of our soul goes from our world to go to another world to talk to the spirits, be they human spirits or animal spirits or whatever. We go to a different place, some people call it underworld, some people call overworld. Whatever, it's a shamanic preference, I suppose. And so, I was at a gateway to that, to that place and I didn't know what it was. So, I was weirded out seriously, but I was also so intrigued because I was thinking that this experience had led me to a crossroads in my life. I knew something was wrong, something was missing. I didn't know what it was, I had no clue, nothing. I mean, my career was OK. I mean, marriage was good and having a child at that time was good. That was all good, but there was a hole still in my heart. I hadn't realized that something wasn't there that was supposed to be there, that I had an itch I couldn't scratch. And at that point in time I was having some real mental health issues. I mean I was having problems with depression and things like that. I was getting these visions of, I worked with adolescents who were sexual offenders and who were also victims of sexual abuse themselves, so I was having visions of the thoughts and feelings they were having, because they would tell their stories and it was like I was there seeing and feeling what they felt and this pain would come home with me. I was very upset a lot of the time and if it hadn't been for Emily, my daughter, and Julia, I don't know what would have happened. What I didn't realize at the time was that I was empathic, which means you pick up other people's feelings. And sometimes you can see things, I guess it's part of being a seer, you can also see those things that had happened in the past. And this is where the whole thing starts here, this is where I start my spiritual path. I walk out of the warrior's dance and I'm just looking around thinking, "I've got to figure this out, I don't know what just happened. I've got to figure this out because I feel more whole now." I wanted to find my way back into this other world because it felt so different, so healing.

So, I just started searching the vendors and craft people looking for what I needed. I wasn't going to walk up to a Native American elder because I was too in awe of them. No, even then I knew without knowing that I shouldn't do that out of the blue. There were all these wonderful native artists and craftspeople there, but this one guy was selling books and that's what I was looking for. So, I just started looking at these books. That's how I deal with things I don't know about. I go read about it first and then I plan a course of action. I needed to find something there and then, but I didn't know what I was looking for.

And so, I looked at all these books and this one just kind of jumped out at me. So, I thought to myself, this one I'm going to take. So, I grabbed the book and thumbed through it for a second. This was it. You know, you just know, you can feel it in your heart. This was my first lesson: When you look to your heart, your heart will tell you what you should do. Not up here in your brain. Your heart tells you because that's where Spirit talks to you. I didn't know it at the time, but Spirit spoke to me and said, "That's the book." So, I picked this book titled *Black Elk Speaks* by John Neidhardt, which is the story of a Lakota Sioux man, a medicine man, who talked to Neidhardt about his life. Neidhardt was actually a poet, but he and Black Elk talked about Custer and what it was like during the wars with the whites. Then he talked about how he was a medicine man and about the Sioux medicine ways, including the seven sacred ceremonies, praying with the pipe, and the story of the White Buffalo Calf Woman who brought the ceremonies and the pipe to the People and taught the People how to pray and how to give thanks to Mother Earth and to grandfather, to Tunkasula. So, I'm reading this, and it was so mesmerizing. I just flew through the book, and when I was finished I felt like my perception of life had changed. This was an amazing path, one that I hoped someday could be my path.

This was my first signpost and it read, "Chris go this way." So, I did. Now, this is what happens when you let the universe know that you're ready: The universe starts opening doors for you. Now the universe tried to contact me before this event, but I wasn't listening, or I wasn't aware enough. Now it finally hit me over the head with a two by four: "Bang! I gotcha!" So, one of the main ways the Lakota pray is with the pipe, chanupa is the name of the sacred pipe, and so I thought that it would be so cool to sit down with some people and smoke the pipe in ceremony like Black Elk had talked about. And so, one day I'm flipping through the Monthly Aspectarian, a metaphysical magazine out of Chicago. It was about an hour and 15 minutes away from Chicago, so it was fairly close to where we lived then. And so, I'm flipping through this magazine and, all of a sudden, I see a list of events, and I start looking through the events and see there is a pipe circle at this place. I think it was called Mind Over Matter. It had the phone number to call. So, I called the phone number and I asked if I could come to their pipe circle and the person said that would be fine. And there it starts. I go there and I meet my first teacher, Claudia Cameron and she taught me the first few things about shamanism and the Lakota way of praying with the pipe and more of their spiritual ways. And that's how this leg of the journey got started for me.

Dave:

This transformation took some time, right? After the pow-wow, you headed home and began to let things soak in. How much time elapsed from the pow-wow before you made the call to attend the pipe circle?

Coyote Chris:

Less than two months.

Dave:

So, over the two months, this is what we were talking about, it happened. So, from nothing to full speed. On the drive home from the pow-wow was your mind already racing about this experience?

Coyote Chris:

I mean, it was the most profound thing that ever happened to me. Yeah, spiritually, I mean, getting married and birth of your children of course are the most important things to me, but this was right up there, and it was just consuming me. It was like. all of a sudden, the door was open and all sorts of things were rushing in, feelings and hope that this may be it, that it would be the thing that I didn't have that I knew I didn't have that I wanted. Maybe this was it. And so, yeah, I had no idea why I had hope, I just knew it felt right and I was consumed by the whole experience.

Dave:

Let's talk about some of your teachers. Who were the people that have influenced you?

Coyote Chris:

So, I had gone through all these things, you know and had my breakthrough, and then I went to the pipe circle. So, I started looking for other experiences and I was with a little group that Claudia was in that did sweat lodges and pipe circles. There needs to be ceremonies and you need to be part of them to get the full experience of the teachings. But I was always looking to expand and there's always more places to go look. That's what you should do. You should never sit with one little group exclusively. I'm not saying you shouldn't stay with them, but you should always go find other teachings. I've seen so many people who say, well, my teacher says I can't do this or read that, or they always seek the same teachers that always tell them the same thing. I never agreed with that. You should try to find other experiences and learn more from other people and so I was always looking for new things to do out there. At Northern Illinois University in Oregon, Illinois, they have this nice little satellite campus out in the woods. So, they had this Native American conference that I signed up for because there was a Sioux author named Ed McGaa, whose Lakota name was Eagle Man, which is Wichasa Wamblee in Sioux, who was going to be there. I had read a book he had written titled *Mother Earth Spirituality* and I had always wanted to meet this man since I'd read it. I had written him a few months before and he had responded and had encouraged me to follow this path. So, I go to meet him, and he was cool, a great guy. I learned some medicine teachings from him and, also, how to make a beaded necklace. It was a great experience, but Spirit wasn't done with me.

While I was walking around the campus one evening, I see this other guy. I'm looking at this guy and my heart tells me I needed to talk to this dude. So later on during the conference, I looked him up and we talked and he told me he was a Mohegan Indian and that he taught psychic divination, Tarot and things like that. His name was Gunn Hollinsworth. Gunn and I talked and the more he explained it the more I felt it was something that I wanted to learn from him. He agreed to teach me and then he asked how I knew I needed to talk to him. I said, "You just had a power, power I could see like light coming off you. And so, I had to talk to you." And this is so important, when you feel like you should talk to somebody, that's what you should do. I didn't know this guy from Adam and just walked up to him. I had enough confidence by then to walk up to him and say, "Hey, we need to talk."

So, he taught me with the Native American Tarot, which is a 78-card deck, and how to do numerology charts. He also taught me some other things as well, including how to mix Tarot and numerology together. He led a pipe circle that I went to sometimes, but he was really good as far as boosting my confidence in my psychic abilities, because that's always been part of me. I just didn't know it. Actually, the first thing I really did was to do psychic work as I learned shamanism, and so, it went in this order: psychic work (my first gig was in 1995 doing Tarot readings in a coffee shop), healing work, and then paranormal investigating – and with the paranormal comes connecting with ghosts, helping people with negative entities, and things like that. I also started to take more of a warrior stance when it came to dealing with entities from the dark. This is how I got started with my spiritual work. Gunn taught me the psychic and how to tap into that and how to trust yourself and to ready yourself to do these things.

Dave:

I know you began your journey by studying and learning as much as you could from the Lakota elders and those influenced by Lakota traditions, but – just like life – you were constantly evolving into spaces where Spirit led you. Finding new teachers contributed insight and new ways of understanding for you. But, before we talk about your Shamanic metamorphosis, I would love it if you could share your story about Sitting Bull's pipe.

Coyote Chris:

At the same conference that I met Ed and Gunn I encountered a man named Jim Gillihan. Jim might've been a quarter Cherokee and he looked like a Norwegian. He had light hair and was a friendly and kind person. Jim had worked for the state of South Dakota and he was like a liaison with the state and the Sioux reservations, with the Lakota. During his duties he had met a medicine man named Frank Fools Crow who was a wicasa wakan, a holy man. Jim actually became a student of Fools Crow's as he had felt the calling to do so and Fools Crow would teach and share with those who had a good heart. (And I guess Jim went off the reservation, so to speak, you know, for his state job, although he was actually on the reservation.) So, Jim just totally immersed himself in Fools Crow's teachings. Now, Fools Crow was the keeper of Sitting Bull's ceremonial chanupa, the actual pipe that Sitting Bull carried. And then came the time when Fools Crow knew it was time to pass it along to a new keeper. He tested various people, including Jim, and at the end of the trials it was Jim who Fools Crow passed the pipe to.

Now, here's a guy who's not Lakota, doesn't have a drop of Lakota blood in him, but he'd been healed from cancer by the pipe and the power of some Lakota medicine people, so that's one thing. Another is that he spoke fluent Lakota, and in the end, it was Spirit who chose him. So, Fools Crow made a decision which I heard upset many people, from my understanding of what Jim told me, on the Lakota reservations and elsewhere, when he gave it to Jim. But I don't think Fools Crow cared what you thought. He knew from Tunkasula (grandfather) and Wakan Tanka (the Great Spirit) where the pipe was supposed to go. So, he passed it to Jim and Jim was a great carrier of that pipe. He would go these ceremonies, doing them flawlessly while speaking fluent Lakota. This white looking guy, you know, he went out and won most everybody's respect and he did have respect. So, I met him at the conference and later on he invited me to come to a place in Indiana where another medicine man lived. And so, I went out to this place to smoke the pipe, do an Inipi ceremony (sweat lodge) and then a vision quest, called a Hambelachya, which means crying for a vision. And so, I get there along with a few other people and we're all kind of waiting around for things to start happening. Now, I knew Jim and that was about it, and so I was hanging around a bunch of strangers.

I have found that a lot of these gatherings can be like this, but it was fine. I mean that everybody is cool as we were all there for the same thing and we had all come with good hearts. Then things got started and Jim brought the pipe out. I'll never forget how it looked, from the wooded stem and pipestone bowl to the eagle feathers. I can't really say a whole lot about it as I don't think I'm supposed to do that, but I'll never forget the weight of it in my hand and it was just amazing. I can feel it today and how profoundly it affected me. I mean, you could just feel the power. Sitting Bull had held it, Crazy Horse had held it, Gall had held it, Fools Crow, had held it, all these great chiefs and warriors of the Lakota. And it was just such a profound experience to hold it, to smoke it and hold it up into the heavens and send the smoke out to Wakan Tanka and the other powers in prayer was just, it was just an amazing experience.

Dave:

And then Spirit moved you in a different direction. Not broader, not more narrow, just different. How would you describe this shift?

Coyote Chris:

Well, I haven't carried a pipe for a while now. For a few years I had my own pipe and walked this path the way I'd been taught. I have a great love and respect for the Lakota medicine ways, but the more I did it, the more I realized it was not the path for me. The way I was taught I wouldn't say was strict, but there are certain things you've got to follow, you know, in certain ways and this has always been difficult for me to do. I also felt that my medicine gift was better suited on another path with my new spirit animal Coyote. In the Lakota tradition there is Iktomi, the spider, who was a trickster and then the Heyoka, the thunder dreamers who are contraries, which can be a difficult life. I knew in my heart, and this is where you have to look in these situations, that I needed the change. It was like I was being told, "Okay, you've done fine, but you need to go someplace else with your medicine." Now this is all on me and not the Lakota path. I had wonderful teachers and I will always be grateful for what I learned.

I felt I was just too eclectic. I like to use different things and I didn't feel like I could do that. And it's like, all the spirits understood. I mean, there's Lakota spirits involved with this and then my spirit guides and there's all these things involved with this whole change. And it wasn't a burden, but I feel like I needed to do something different to properly respect the Lakota way. I needed to put that to the side because I would not do it the way I was supposed to. I knew I would not. Now this decision came during a time when Julia and I had decided to move back to our hometown of Alton, IL, with Emily and her brother Max, who was a year old when we returned. We went through the process of finding jobs, a home and getting the kids in school and daycare. We had been back a month or two when I happened to look in the paper, the Alton Telegraph, and I read that there was an event at Southern Illinois University-Edwardsville, which is not too far from where we lived. The ad stated that Johnny Moses (Nootka/Tulalip), who lived near Seattle, was going to be there teaching about the Si-Si Wiss Medicine Tradition from the Pacific Northwest Coast, I looked at it and right there my heart jumped. I said to myself, "I gotta go." It was on a Saturday and it was nasty out that weekend, sleet and rain coming down. But I went down there to listen about this medicine tradition that I had never heard about and I was glad I did. There I met Johnny, and local people who were in the Red Cedar Circle, of which I am now a part, that met at the university as well. After listening to Johnny's teachings and hearing the Si-Si Wiss songs, I knew that this was it. I felt that I would feel more comfortable to do my medicine without breaking with a tradition and that it was more of a fit for me and I felt very much at home with it. Because very basically, it's more like you act as Spirit moves you, and Dave, you've seen the backpack I carry with me whenever I get anywhere near doing any kind of medicine work or anything like that. I carry that as I can do whatever I need to do out of that backpack. I can do healing work. I do spiritual work. I can do paranormal work, I do psychic work, readings and the like. I keep all these spiritual tools in my backpack because I never know what I'm going to need do when I get there. Spirit tells me what to do when I get there.

Dave:

Do you think there are parallels between the Unitarian traditions of your childhood and the Si-Si Wiss tradition you discovered along your journey?

Coyote Chris:

It's definitely more similar. I mean, the humanist Unitarians would say, well, you know, the spiritual part would be bunk, but your good acts would be indicative of your growth as a person without the help of God or Spirit. However, there are many spiritual Unitarians as well, who would say that they are more open to the various spiritual or mystical paths. So probably my upbringing did influence me towards the Si-Si Wiss medicine, but also my personality as I like to do different things and not everything the same way every time. And you know, I probably could have gotten that point on the Lakota path. I imagine where I could have done that sort of thing, but the Si-Si Wiss path was certainly more open to me and has allowed me to be more eclectic because like I said, Spirit tells me what to do when I get there. And that's how I prefer to act, and the Si-Si Wiss tradition gives me enough of a framework and base to work from. I just need a little bit and that's what it provides me. Whereas other traditions have lot more intricacies, you have to follow these steps and things like that. Now the SI-Si Wiss tradition has ways to do things, but these ways work well for me.

Dave:

I know your relationship with Johnny has continued to grow and develop over the years and he has returned to Southern Illinois several times. Would you characterize your relationship with him today as more of a friendship than a mentor/protégé relationship?

Coyote Chris:

I would think so. Yeah. I mean, we don't see each other a whole lot. He lives in California, Northern California, now. He is, as I said earlier, originally from the Seattle area in the Pacific Northwest and up through there. The teacher thing is probably more predominant, but I think over the years our relationship has become closer. I went many years without seeing him. He came here in the early 1990s, in the later 1990s, and maybe 2001. He didn't make it here for quite a while. But he's been here a couple of times over the past few years and when he comes back now, I'm usually the one who picks him up at the airport. Another medicine person named Kathy Sundown has been travelling with him, and she is someone I admire and learn from as well, and we'll do stuff like go to the dollar store. Johnny likes to go to the dollar store or maybe the grocery store before he checks in at his hotel and it's fun to do those things with him and we have good time. So yeah, I would say now, we are closer than we were before.

He's closer to my friend Greg Fields. Greg is a philosophy professor at SIUE, where I first saw Johnny, and Greg is the one that brought the Red Cedar Circle to this area and so he has been working with Johnny for some time now. Greg is actually writing a book about Johnny that's coming out before too long and so if you see a book out there about Johnny Moses by Dr. Greg Fields, that's definitely going to be worth the read because I mean Johnny is an amazing, amazing man. Now he has his faults, but we all do, and so we trust the medicine that the Creator has given us and do our best, because nobody is perfect. So much of this medicine path is about finding what your medicine is. We all have medicine, everybody has a gift from God, from Spirit and that's our medicine. Now a lot of people make errors when it comes to these gifts, in that instead of healing themselves and getting themselves straight first, like I was taught, they go out to try and help others while still carrying all their emotional baggage with them. This emotional baggage gets in the way of the spiritual energy that flows through them and it won't work as well.

I had to get myself straight when I started this because, like I

mentioned, I was depressed and had lots of issues. I needed to deal with those, which I did before I could really, truly start helping people with my medicine. The bottom line is that you can't really help heal others if you still need a lot of healing yourself. So, in the Si-Si Wiss tradition the first thing you do is to pray for your medicine and you find your medicine and you work with it to heal yourself first, as you learn about how to use it, it helps heal you. And then, once you accomplish that, then you're ready to go out and help other people. Does it mean you're fixed forever and perfect? No, but you're more aware of what's going on inside you. I got to keep an eye on myself on certain things. So, any medicine person, and any other person for that matter, who says their psyches are perfect and that they have all their little duckies in a row are giving you bullshit. You know it is. I mean you got to keep an eye on yourself because there is always some situation out there looking to drag you down.

Dave:

Tell me about your evolution. From the moment you set foot down at the pow-wow, to the first pipe circle, to meeting Johnny Moses – over that time you are studying, learning and developing your understanding of the world around you and beginning to accept the role Spirit has carved out for you – how many years passed before the Coyote Chris Sutton we know today emerged?

Coyote Chris:

Let's see, I've been doing shamanism for 26 years as of this year. Probably the Lakota path for probably four to five years and then the switch. So, I'd done that for several years and then I switched to the Si-Si Wiss path I follow now, but I was inactive in the Red Cedar Circle for a while. I'm active now, but as you know, life catches up with you sometimes. At one point I didn't go circle for a few years because Emily and Max were both playing on sports teams from elementary school through high school. So, I was coaching soccer and all these other park and rec sports and things like that for them. While I did miss my involvement with Red Cedar, I think these things happened for a reason and I think that reason was that I needed to learn how to stand on my own two feet, to learn to strengthen my personal relationship with Spirit.

Dave:

That is exactly what I want to focus on. Over the course of many years, you must have struggled to come to grips with what was happening to you from spiritual, emotional and philosophical perspectives. As your faith transformed you, your spirit transformed as you developed your own medicine as a shaman. What were the outward appearances of this transformation? When did Chris Sutton, upstanding member of the Riverbend community with a wife, two kids and a home, become comfortable publicly as Coyote Chris Sutton, shaman, paranormal investigator, intuitive healer and spiritual counselor and advisor?

Coyote Chris:

Not for a long time I didn't. It was difficult because when I first moved back home, I thought I had to be like what I thought a medicine man should be, you know? And my perception was to that I had to be perfect in this, I could not drink, be stoic, and things like that. You know me, I like to have a drink and I have no moral objection to it, so I was trying to be somebody who I wasn't, and that's not what it's about. It's not being somebody you're not, it's adding to what you are and changing things that aren't good for you, but never throwing yourself away. People that get in this way, throw themselves away, because some of them are not being genuine, not being themselves. And I can say that because that's what I was doing, I can look back and say I was not being genuine. I was trying to do the right thing, I wasn't, you know, trying to be a jerk or anything, but I thought I had to act in a certain way. And so I got out of that, but then I run into to this situation where, okay, I have two younger children and they love their dad, I know that, but they don't want to have the "weird dad" and this happens to a lot of people who have a shamanic or metaphysical practice of some sort. So, I've got this problem where Julia was okay with my practice. I mean, it took some time for that to evolve between us as she wasn't too keen on it at first, but for the kids having a weird dad would have been difficult socially for them as other kids, and adults, can be cruel about that sort of thing. No child wants to go to school and hear that their father was in league with Satan because he spoke to spirits.

Now, I understood that. Not that they didn't think what I did was cool, they did, but it's like, "Dad," Emily was really good at this, "Dad you know if people knew that you did that and you know..." and I said, "Yeah, I understand." And I did and I was fine with keeping a low profile. So, I would do all my work in St. Louis. I would do a lot of psychic fairs and events like that over there. And then eventually my friend, Sandy Little Lizard, opened up a metaphysical shop in a town north of Alton and I did psychic fairs and taught classes there for many years. She and I did work together, and it was far enough away and out of the local spotlight where people, especially possible local muggles wouldn't notice (I love Jo Rowling) what I was up to.

During this time, I was still gaining strength and I was still gaining acceptance of who I was. I started to accept that a shamanic practitioner was who I was, because before then I doubted myself and doubted the wisdom of Spirit for gifting me. I would say, "Why me? Why the hell do you want me? Why me?" And many who walk these types of paths ask themselves, why they get this gift. So, it took quite a while before I decided to stop worrying about that and just go ahead and do it. I'm not any more special than anybody else, this is just the way it happened, so I had to live with myself and accept that I was different. I always knew I was different even when I was young. I knew I was different; I just didn't how I was different.

It took me a long time to figure that kind of stuff out. So, I go through all this, I go through this time and I'm still getting my act together and I feel better about everything. And finally, I was doing a gig here in town as I was helping Sharyn Luedke, who owns the McPike Mansion, with her yearly camp out as I had done for several years without any fanfare. But on this occasion, there was an article about the camp out in the Alton paper and in the article, it mentioned that shaman Coyote Chris Sutton would also be in attendance at this year's camp out. So, my daughter is sitting there and I got the paper out and I said, "Emily, cat's out of the bag, babe." By then, Emily was in high school and Max was in middle school. and so, it was okay. Now, of course, many of their friends think it's cool that Emily and Max's dad does these things and it's a total reversal what it was before. Now our whole family has done spiritual and paranormal events together over the past few years or so, for which I'm very happy about.

Also, about this time I made my first television appearance. I did a little thing on *Ghost Lab*, which starred Brad and Barry Klinge, which was on the Discovery Channel in 2008 and 2009. They were investigating the McPike Mansion for the show and Sharyn had invited me and Sandy Little Lizard and others to stop by while they were shooting. So, I was happily hanging out watching everything when the producer wanted some local investigators to be interviewed so I got on there for like 30 seconds when the episode aired ("If Walls Could Talk, Part II"). I must admit it was pretty cool to see.

Well, then about three years later I got a call out of the blue from the producer of *The Dead Files: Revisited* and she said they needed a shaman to come up and do a house cleansing at this family home up in Rock Island, IL. It was a place that Steve

DiSchiavi and Amy Allan had investigated in the original Dead Files episode that the *Revisited* episode was following up on that. The producer said she found my name on a shaman internet list and saw that I lived in Illinois and asked how far away I was? Now I'm like four hours away from Rock Island, but I said, "Don't worry about how far I am. I'll be there. I can get off work." So, I went to Rock Island and filmed the episode ("Evil Underground and Killed by the Klan") in March of 2013. It seemed like doors were opening for me in ways that I hadn't thought about.

Dave:

So, once you let the Coyote out of the bag, it was a bit of a blast in so many directions. You quickly moved from house cleansings to television shows. Of all of the hats you were wearing – psychic, healer, medium, storyteller or paranormal investigator – which one fit you best?

Coyote Chris:

It's all of them. It's not about juggling, it's all part of being one. All the pieces finally got together and it's just... we're all multifaceted people in very different ways. I mean some people can fix plumbing, but I can't, but I can sit down and do a spiritual reading with you and help you out that way. But it's just all part of me. It's all, everything that I do fits under the shaman umbrella and everything I do flows from that. My relationship with Spirit is through my medicine path.

Dave:
Is there one particular role which feels more natural?

Coyote Chris:
Maybe so. Do I like doing certain things more? Maybe sometimes, just as there are skills I tend to use less. I'm always

kind of like that with healing work. I do it and I have confidence in myself, but I find myself doing that less. I like working with other medicine people when I do that. I like working with your wife Donna a lot because, part of my medicine, or my gift, is sort of destructive in a way, but in a good way. If you're doing healing work with people, you've got to break up the negative energy that is clinging to them. I've got my Thunderbird here with the clouds and the lightning that my friend Jeremy Baker did for me (pointing to Thunderbird tattoo on his arm) and this represents that positive destructive energy that I use when doing healing. So, I like doing healing work with someone who knows Reiki with me or something similar for a nice balance of healing energy. I can do solo healing work, but I do have this preference, though. I like to go through and break away the old stuff, the old negative energy. We have these deposits of negative energy in and on our bodies and it's these deposits that cause sickness. I like to bust those out and have somebody like Donna come in and put in the nice, calm, quiet, good healing energy and good things like that. It creates such a positive balance in the person receiving the healing. So, I guess I feel like I'm not called do more one than the other. No, not necessarily. I think I can step up to anything I need to, but I do have preferences. In the end, however, it's Spirit's call.

Dave:

How do you find balance in your life? We talked about your evolution over the last 30 years. You've raised two children. You have a great marriage. You are enjoying a successful career with your full-time employer. But, now you're coming up at a time in your life where you're still working professionally and you are also Coyote Chris Sutton. And the shaman-side of your life is not part-time, it absolutely consumes you 24/7. This is who you are. How do you find balance in life?

Coyote Chris:

I did. I finally did. And it took me so long to do it. I am Coyote Chris, no matter where I go, and by believing that I have learned to accept it. Now, on my day job, do I pull out the drum and start singing? No, I don't do that. That's not appropriate unless they ask me to. I have done drumming at nursing homes before for residents and I've given talks at our facility about my spiritual path. I am an advocate, an Ombudsman, for elders in long-term care facilities and my office is in the local senior center. And so, I've done that type of thing in a teaching sort of way, but normally it's not acceptable in the workplace. But, you know, having that mindset that I'm always Coyote Chris, is more genuine than trying to separate them. I used to try to have one mindset where I was just Chris, and then distanced the other part of me, the Coyote part, which is my spiritual self away from me. That was a mistake on my part as I was walking around not totally being my true self. So, now don't go to work and turn it off like I used to.

I don't go to a concert and turn it off. I'm always me because, pardon me, it's who I am. It's like if you're a good musician and you know that's always part of you, but you don't break out the Fender Stratocaster and start wailing while you're at work or standing in line at the grocery store. You don't do that, but you're always a musician. That's who you always are and it's the same thing with this. Actually, everyone is pretty good about it at work. Once my boss took my name plate with Chris Sutton on it, flipped it over and wrote Coyote Chris on the back with black marker and stuck it back on my door. I used to keep it a secret, but no secrets anymore. This is who I am.

Dave:

I want to go back to something that you described earlier, specifically when you were talking about how Spirit chose you. Many people are confused about the concept of Spirit. From a Western, Christian perspective, they often connote that Spirit means you saw the Holy Ghost and the Holy Ghost came over you and said, "Chris, this is the direction I want you to go in." But, you are talking about Spirit in terms of spirit guidance and emotional influence. Was that a difficult calling to understand?

Coyote Chris:

You're talking about the Holy Spirit and before we get on to the effect Spirit has on people, I want to acknowledge Christian mysticism. I read some books by Thomas Merton, who was a

Catholic author and was a monastic, a monk. And the way he talks about how the mystery of his faith shows that there is, in some Christian traditions, some pretty healthy mysticism there. That's very similar to what we have been talking about where the Holy Spirit's actually doing the same thing in calling mystics into service. However, you don't hear too much about it anymore. Merton wrote about the Gnostics and some of these Catholic mystics like St. John of the Cross and Theresa of Avila and he compared his ideas of mysticism to some forms of Buddhism. You know, these Christian mystics are really into the same type of spiritual thing that I'm into, of how Spirit interacts with us. They were amazing. But unfortunately, most Christians, that I have seen, don't commune with God that way much. I wish they would because there are some marvelous, mystical traditions in the Christian faith. Now, as far as how it interacts with a person, I think that the Holy Spirit acts on people the way Spirit and spirit guides have acted on me. It's just a different path to the same source.

I do this meditation exercise that you and Donna have done with me before called Becoming a Hollow Bone. It's where we draw energy from the earth and from the sky and we breathe our way into a kind of meditative state that allow us to become a hollow bone, a bone that the energy and will of Spirit goes through. This is what grandpa Fools Crow taught us as he shared this with many people including some who taught me. And this energy actually flows through you and you can feel it. So, I was just talking earlier about how I don't know what I'm going to do when I'm called to do spiritual work until I get there. When I'm ready to get going I make myself a hollow bone and then I connect with Spirit and It tells me what to do. It's like during this communion you are given a plan and then you're ready to go. Now when you are a hollow bone the message comes through your heart, not your brain. Gunn taught me this saying: "Your brain is a wonderful tool, but a lousy master because it will lie to you" And it does, as your brain is bogged down with you looking back at your past and ahead at your future and it acts as if it can't be bothered by the present.

And so, you listen to your heart. This is where spirit comes to talk to you. Not in your brain, that's where the message becomes muddied and diluted because your old tapes from your past are playing and your mind is demanding that you overthink every idea and insists on a risk assessment for everything you do. That doesn't happen in your heart where you take the message in and just go with it. It comes to you and you feel it, like intuition, so you get the feeling and an idea coalesces in your mind very briefly and then you have the message. This is Spirit telling you what you need to do and you do it. So, that's one-way Spirit speaks to you. Spirit also speaks to you through your spirit guides. Now a question that so many people have is how do I meet my spirit guides? Well, there's all kinds of ways. The thing is to be open to them contacting you. You've got to tell them you ready to meet them and that you're willing to work with them. They're not here just to, to beat you over the head to get your attention and share all this divine wisdom with you. You have to work at it.

This path takes work. It's a lot of work, but gosh it's so worth it. I have spirit guides, my great, great grandmother is a spirit guide of mine and there's a couple others. I can't really say who they are, as these relationships are very sacred. One helps me with healing, and another helps me with protection when I go into the dark to to see what negative things are lurking around bothering people in their houses and on their land.

Dave:

Setting this aside, talking about perhaps the living or those who aren't living, who are some of your other influences?

Coyote Chris:

Bill Coty. Bill was living here in the area for a few months, but he's back in the Seattle area now where his home is. Bill has been practicing the Si-Si Wiss medicine tradition for many years and his knowledge is incredible. Now, he was here helping Greg Fields work on his book about Johnny Moses, as Bill has known Johnny for a long time. He is a very big inspiration to me because when I started coming back to the Red Cedar Circle, he was there, and he taught me, and the rest of the circle, a lot about the Si-Si Wiss tradition I didn't know. He taught us about spirit travelling to medicine chants, prophecies, and healing work. Plus, he is a great guy who will always help you.

The books I've read have influenced me a lot. I'm talking about people who I've never met as well, but they were a big part of my journey as well. The teachings of the Buddha gave helped me stay focused in the present. I'm very influenced by the Tao Te Ching, which introduced me to Taoism. Taoism helps me simplify my thoughts when they become too many and jumbled. Not many people know, but I've been very influenced by Eastern philosophy, specifically Buddhism and especially Tibetan Buddhism. The Dalai Lama has been an inspiration to me and so many people. He is a true holy person. Joseph Campbell, who wrote the "Hero with a Thousand Faces where he takes myths from so many cultures that give the same messages and forms them into a pathway through life. He called it the Hero's Journey and it's a path that we all walk anytime we're on a spiritual path or a journey through to find your bliss. So, Campbell and his writings really influenced me by getting me to look deeper into myths and stories. Other people I read about that influenced me were Mad Bear Anderson, who was a Tuscaroran medicine man and Rolling Thunder, who was a healer, environmentalist, and teacher. Now there were characters in fiction that influenced me as well, like Merlin and Alec Guinness' Obi-Wan Kenobi These are the teachers I found in books and movies that influenced me to expand my thinking on how to use my medicine.

Dave:

I really feel compelled to say that one of the most fascinating things about you is lineage. Time moves in linear fashion and your development and understanding of Spirit occurred over time, but your development is also richly nebulous. Mentors who guided you, influencers who encouraged you, authors you studied, traditions you learned from your father as a child, all of this makes perfect sense. And it overlaps each other. Maybe the content of the literature changed, but the formula and methodology in the way knowledge came to you was consistent. I really appreciate your empirical approach, because it is concrete and can help others along their paths as you point to real, tangible experiences, books and people. You had to build a sturdy foundation of knowledge. Your transformation didn't happen overnight.

Coyote Chris:

No, and I think it's a shame because a lot of people don't read. I mean, it opens you up to so many teachings as you can only meet so many people. I have talked a lot of different people and learned from these different people, but your ability to see people in person is not infinite. Fools Crow is dead. He died in 1989. Rolling Thunder is dead. Mad Bear Anderson is dead. I've talked to different medicine people and they were very helpful. But to me, you've got to go outside those boundaries, and you read about people or you read what they've written, in the case of Campbell. So yeah, to me, it's very important as a way to learn.

Dave:

I think too reading takes effort. If it's an active thing, you don't just sit there and absorb the knowledge. You don't just go someplace. And because you're in the company of somebody or you participated in something, maybe halfheartedly, it doesn't transform you to become something different. You actually had to go out and actively pursue the knowledge that you obtained over the years to transform yourself.

Coyote Chris:

Oh, I've got folders at home with notes I've jotted down about the teachings I've encountered on my path. I have a folder that has "Quotes" written on it and I've got all sorts of things in there, all these little sayings. Rumi is in there and the Buddha and Jesus, even. You know, Jesus had some really great teachings. If you view Jesus as a shaman, he's the greatest hands down, a mystic of the highest degree. He was an avatar, an amazing self-actualized teacher who tried to teach people how to love one another. And you know, he was something else. He taught us we should love our neighbors as we love ourselves. That had never been said before he did. And he was quite right. So, he is an inspiration for me as well, even though I'm not a Christian.

Dave:

Tell me your elevator speech. You have 30 seconds to ride in an elevator to the top of a 100-story building with anyone in history – who would it be and what would you tell them?

Coyote Chris:

Fools Crow.

Dave:

What would you talk about?

Coyote Chris:

I don't know. I'd know when I got there. I don't try to plan for most things. But I'm sure I would enjoy the experience. Speaking of people I'd like to meet, I put a tweet out, oh gosh, it's been a year or so and I posted that there are the two people I wanted to meet in person. I mean, these people are still alive so I could meet them in the flesh today if I were fortunate. The first one is His Holiness the Dalai Lama, the other one is Dave Grohl. Now people might think that is a weird dichotomy. Well, you know, obviously, I've met holy people, but I mean, the Dalai Lama is one person that I just would love to meet. I watch him sometimes online and his speeches and his teachings of the Dharma are so enlightening. He's such a kind soul, a gentle soul and he talks to us about not being attached to things. That is so important, because we attach ourselves to other people and material things and that causes suffering. I've worked with so many people who are so attached to the past, attached to this material thing, attached to that relationship. I know people whose lives are tormented by people who are in the grave and they still let those people mess their lives up because they're attached to what that person, often a parent, said or did to them in the past. These memories sometimes make their life a living hell and they just won't let go of them. So that's why I spend a lot of time talking to people about that when I'm teaching, about letting things go. That definitely comes from Buddhism.

Now, Dave Grohl, and it may sound like a weird thing to put him next to the Dalai Lama, but the guy puts himself out there as who he is and reminds others to be who they are. He's a contemporary figure who doesn't sell out, he appears to be who he is all the time that I can tell and not only that, but he preaches it. If you listen to him, he preaches the very thing that a lot of holy people preach. If you want to be the best at what you do it takes time. It takes work. But go do it and be who you are. I remember a message he gave to aspiring musicians in a rant about *American Idol* and *The Voice*:

"When I think about kids watching a TV show like American Idol or The Voice, then they think, 'Oh, OK, that's how you become a musician, you stand in line for eight fucking hours with 800 people at a convention center and... then you sing your heart out for someone and then they tell you it's not fuckin' good enough.' Can you imagine?" he implores. "It's destroying the next generation of musicians! Musicians should go to a yard sale and buy an old fucking drum set and get in their garage and just suck. And get their friends to come in and they'll suck, too. And then they'll fucking start playing and they'll have the best time they've ever had in their lives and then, all of a sudden, they'll become Nirvana. Because that's exactly what happened with Nirvana. Just a bunch of guys that had some shitty old instruments and they got together and started playing some noisy-ass shit, and they became the biggest band in the world. That can happen again! You don't need a fucking computer or the internet or *The Voice* or *American Idol*." - Dave Grohl, *The Toronto Globe and Mail*, May 7, 2013

It's the same for those of us who walk a shamanic or some other metaphysical path, because you have to work on becoming your true self and to learn your practice and find your medicine. It doesn't come on the wings of chariots where all of a sudden, you're some kind of master. You have to work and sweat and go through the same things over and over again, just like learning to play music. And never listen to those who say you can't do it, that you're not good enough. They will always be there to judge you, just like on *American Idol*, so don't fall into their trap. Follow your heart and keep plugging away.

You just don't go to a place and listen for one hour a week and be saved. That's not what this is about. This is about actually trying to better your soul, better yourself through your spiritual path. And by doing that and then helping other people around you means so much. Because the better person you are, the better person you make other people, whether you know them or not. It is so important to do that. And then, so these are the type of people where one looks like he's the guy from everyday life and just a musician, like Grohl, to one of the most exalted holy persons in the world. But they're both doing their jobs. They're being who they are, and they are affecting people positively because they use their voices this way. And that's big stuff spiritually for anyone when they can help other people grow.

Dave:

Fast forward years from now. You are dead. What's the opening line at your funeral?

Coyote Chris:

I never thought of that. I hope they say that I had integrity. I think that's the main thing, because if that is true, then I was able to affect people when I needed to. You know what means a lot to me is to have integrity. I think when you lose integrity you're lost. I don't give a shit what you know, who you know, because if people don't believe that you're good enough, that you can't follow through on who you are, then you've lost it.

Dave:

What keeps you up at night now? Not the Chris Sutton of 30 years ago – children, wife, mortgage, retirement – but Coyote Chris Sutton of 2020.

Coyote Chris:

It doesn't happen often. I will say that's such a change in my life because I used to lay awake and worry and ponder things. I don't do that so much anymore. Usually when I go to bed, I've accepted the day and I've accepted everything that came with it. That's another benefit of doing this spiritual thing is that you tend to kind of let things go. There's a way of looking at things which I believe is a Toltec way of identifying what is important and what is not. I read about this it in an old Carlos Castaneda book where the sorcerer Don Juan supposedly gave him this teaching, that your death was your best adviser. Look at the problems in your life and compare them to your death. Why are you worried about a leaky roof when death is in the shadows, waiting?

So next to dying is a money problem important? No, it's not, because I got another day tomorrow, hopefully, to rectify a wrong or to do something better. But if I don't, then I go to sleep having done the best I can. I don't lay awake at night very much and worry, because worry won't change a thing, The one thing I do worry about is time, but I'm not afraid of dying. That happens to us all, but I do think about whether I am I going to get everything accomplished I'm supposed to. That's what worries me. Because I don't know what the end result is supposed to be, you know? If I did, I would know what needed to be done and I could retire from it. But in my mind, that's not how it works. Right now, I'm not too far from retirement age as far as my regular job goes, but I was telling a friend of mine the other day: "You know? I can't wait to retire so I can go to work full time." I sincerely mean that I don't see an end to this. I'm not going to say one day, "Okay, my spiritual work is done." I don't ever think it's ever going to be done. The only thing I worry about is will I be able to get everything done.

Dave:
You'll know when you get there.

Coyote Chris:
Yeah. I guess when I get to the next realm, to Spirit, I'll know. So, that's the only thing that worries me. We have to understand that our life ends in death, no matter what, and you have to be ready for that.

Dave:

What makes you happy?

Coyote Chris:

Oh, lots of things made me happy. Sitting here talking to you makes me happy. Being with my children and my wife and my friends makes me happy. Going to baseball games makes me happy. See, I still like all that stuff. Also, I like football, I watch football and baseball, and hockey.

Dave:

Shamans like football? I can think of a few teams that might be interesting in putting you on retainer if it might help their chances!

Coyote Chris:

They can like anything they want to. You know what I mean? You don't have to give everything up for your spiritual path. If it's something you enjoy, then you're still being you. I like going to Circle. I like singing songs. I love giving presentations. I love talking about what I do and what I know. Oh, and about the things I can share things to people that will help them out. I love, being in front of people, I'm a big show off. I love to get up and talk to people.

Dave:

Without using names, who is the one person you remember over the course of your spiritual journey who was so profoundly impacted by your counsel that their experience could not be categorized as anything less than transformational?

Coyote Chris:

You know, I can think of several people. Usually it's in a small way, in a smaller sense that I'm affected. You do work with people and you don't know quite how much you've helped them until they come up a year or two later and say, "Thank you so much. What you told me really, really worked," or, "Your healing just really worked," or, "What you did really worked." It made me see things differently. When you see somebody that that you helped walking their spiritual path it is such a great feeling.

I love this one story because I didn't intend any of it to happen. I was helping out at the McPike Mansion, like I do here at the Mineral Springs, and I was doing some paranormal tours for the guests. There we take people down into the basement and we go into a little wine cellar down there that has a vaulted limestone ceiling and a dirt floor. Everybody sits and we call the spirits to come join us. There's a family of ghosts there, Henry McPike and some of his family, and they seem to like the company, so they come in to visit with the guests. So, on this occasion I was with my friend Sandy Little Lizard, and we two shaman folks were guiding the tours.

Now there are a couple of spirits in this place who will latch on to people who are fledgling empaths, those who can feel other people's feelings. And these ghosts love to play with empaths by putting their sad feelings into them and getting them upset. People who don't know that they're empaths are really susceptible to this because they don't know how to protect themselves. There are a lot of ghosts out there roaming around and most are real nice and not evil or malevolent, but some are just jerks, you know, and they like to mess with people. And so, in this particular instance, we had 30 people down there and Sandy's on one end of the wine cellar and I'm at the other end and we're teaching our guests how to recognize some of the ways that ghosts show themselves. After that we asked that the McPike spirits to join us and tell other spirits who might be hanging around that they are welcome if they are of the Light. You don't want to invite the negative entities that bear ill will as they can spoil the party. Then we turn the lights out and go into a dark room session in the pitch blackness and out come the ghosts appearing as sparkly lights and shapes that are darker than dark. After a few minutes, a lady next to Sandy began to feel something touching her and she became afraid. Sandy began bringing in her medicine, her spirit power, to help her get the ghost off her.

In any type of situation like this you always bring in Spirit for energy and guidance. So, Sandy working with her and doing the medicine, sending the lady energy to try to help her get through this. And so, after a couple of minutes go by a lady on my end starts becoming affected. She started feeling sad and scared, so I get my medicine pulled up and I start sending her energy to help her. So, Sandy and I are doing this at opposite ends of the cellar and people watched it the best they could or just listened. And all of a sudden, a woman in the middle of the room calls out and says, "Wow. I saw a flash of light!"

Now this happens a lot in these dark room sessions as spirits often come as flashes of light, so we don't think too much of it. And so, we keep doing our medicine and finally the session's over and we get everybody put back together again, and they're feeling better. So, we come out of the cellar and this lady comes up to us and she says, "I can see!" and Sandy and I are saying, "What are you talking about?" I asked her if she was the one that saw the flash and she said yes and then she goes on to tell us that she had lost much of her eyesight due to disease over the past few years. Then she tells us that she can now see things she couldn't before she went into the wine cellar. I was stunned and nearly in tears because it was so cool and she was so happy. We had no idea about her when we brought Spirit into the room, but Spirit acts as it needs to and, "BAM!" the energy goes to this lady and heals her eyes.

I was kind of thinking that, well, maybe it's just a little gift from Spirit to her that would last a while so she could see her grandchildren better, or something like that. And so. Sandy and I are back at the same event a year later and there this lady is. She comes up and gives each of us a big hug and then we started talking. She told us that she had gone to her doctor and he glanced at her file and examined her eyes. The doctor looked at her file again and stated that they must have given him the wrong file as this couldn't be you. "What do you mean?" she said. "This is me." She was then told that her vision had improved to 20/20 and also that all the scar tissue from her previous 11 surgeries was gone and she could see perfectly normal. We had brought the medicine and a miracle happened. A year later and it was still holding good. I've never been so amazed in my life, and it was not about me, and Sandy will tell you the same thing that it had nothing to do with us. We just brought it in. But it's the most amazing thing that I've ever seen happen and it was not by intention. It just happened because we brought Spirit there.

Dave:

If you had a bumper sticker what would it read?

Coyote Chris:

It would say "Coyote Chris Sutton: Bringing Light to the Darkest Places." That's kind of my tagline. What it means is that whether the darkness is in somebody's heart, or mind, or if it's in their house, I just show up with my backpack and I go try to bring light to wherever it needs to be. And I don't worry about it. I don't get scared. You and I have been in some hairy places, you know, where it's been scary. I've been in the sub-basement here at the Mineral Springs with my son Max and we heard two sets of footsteps circling around us in the pitch black. You and I have come across an entity here that tried to grab us. There are all sorts of scary things out there. But when you bring in the light with you, you have to trust that and I do trust it This paves the way for me to experience these cool things that happen because I trust it and I trust myself.

Spirit puts me where I need to be, so I have to have great trust in spirit, but I have to have greater trust in me. You have to trust yourself with your medicine, with who you are. And the beauty of this whole thing is that I've gained more trust in myself as a human being since I've been walking this path and that's why it's so important. That's why I spend all this time trying to let people in on this stuff. I'm not evangelizing or anything like that, but you know when you hear me talk, you're going to hear this stuff. You're going to hear that you've got medicine. You're going to hear that you can heal yourself with your medicine. And you're going to hear that you can take this medicine, this gift, that every one of us has, and help somebody else with it. That's exactly what you're going to hear. So yeah, bringing light to the darkest places.

# PART II

# WALK

*the*

# PATH

# Part 2

## *Walk the Path*

Dave:

This part of the book focuses on the spiritual gifts of Coyote Chris Sutton. Folks may have seen Chris' appearances on several paranormal television shows, as well as his own internet broadcast on Vidispace. He is well-known on the paranormal travel circuit and has been investigating the Mineral Springs Hotel here in Alton, Illinois, for several years. When you combine Chris' transformation as detailed in the last edition along with his pursuits of the paranormal and spiritual, you really end up with a compelling story of a man who is walking his spiritual path. And that is the focus of this book -- how he investigates, heals, conducts himself as a medium and, most importantly, how his path as a shaman impacts all that he does. Welcome back to Mineral Springs, Chris.

Coyote Chris:

Dave, it's always great to be here, as you know. I love being here and investigating and hanging out with you and your lovely wife Donna and the great crew here and all the great events we've had together. So, it's always a pleasure to be sitting down with you.

Dave:

I think the most recent thing you have been involved with is a benefit you hosted for Mauna Kea here at the Mineral Springs Hotel. Can you tell us a little bit about why you got involved in that effort?

Coyote Chris:

Sure. On the Island of Hawaii is Mauna Kea, the highest mountain there, and it's one of the most holy places in Hawaii. You've known me for several years now and you know that one of the things that I'm interested in is preserving nature and also preserving places that are sacred to the native folks that live there, not the colonists, but the Native Americans, the first people who were here long before the Europeans. And I got very interested in Mauna Kea because I read about the Ku Kai'i Mauna, the Native Hawai'ian protectors of Mauna, who are trying to stop a large telescope from being built on the mountain itself. They are so peaceful and they walk their talk of peaceful protest. And it's just such a beautiful thing to watch when they're together at the base of Mauna Kea singing the songs that they have sung for centuries and doing dances and songs together that they call "protocol." Jason Mamoa, you know, Aquaman, shows up in a video I watched wearing a lei po'o (a traditional headdress) and Hawaiian regalia. He crouched down and sort of duck walks to an elder with a gift and they greet each other.

I was struck by the greeting. The elder took Jason by the head and pressed his forehead to Jason's and they talked quietly for a while before Jason presented the elder with the gift. Powerful stuff! But what really motivated me to have a benefit for the protectors of Mauna Kea was that one night I was reaching out into Spirit towards Mauna Kea. How this works is hard to describe. Some people might call it praying, but to me it's communing, but prayer and communion are the same thing to me. I'm trying to reach out with my energy with the energy of the person or place I'm trying to connect with. So, when I went outside to commune one night, I put my thumbs and my forefingers together, the sign given to show you support Mauna and I reached out to her. I sent out my energy to give whatever little energy one can give to something so great as a gift and a sign of greeting. What I felt back was this incredible, loving energy that dwarfed me, and I felt the slightest brush across my cheek. And when the communion was finished, I was overwhelmed.

Dave:

Overwhelmed? From a physical, spiritual, or emotional perspective?

Coyote Chris:

Oh, I was in tears. I really was. And it was one of the greatest things that ever happened in my spiritual life. And it came at a time where I was just wanting to offer a prayer and my hope and my love to Mauna Kea and the native Hawai'ian people. I saw where the people say, Mauna told me this and Mauna told me that, and I totally believe them. Because, I mean, she didn't talk to me, but she brushed me, and it was one of the most incredible experiences I've ever had.

Dave:

I really think there is much greater awareness of mankind's connection to Mother Earth nowadays. This awakening has definitely reached a much broader audience of people over the past few years and you have many physical representations of that awareness on your body – and by physical, I am talking about your tattoos. I'm not going to call you a billboard (pointing at Chris' tattoos), but you do practice what you preach.

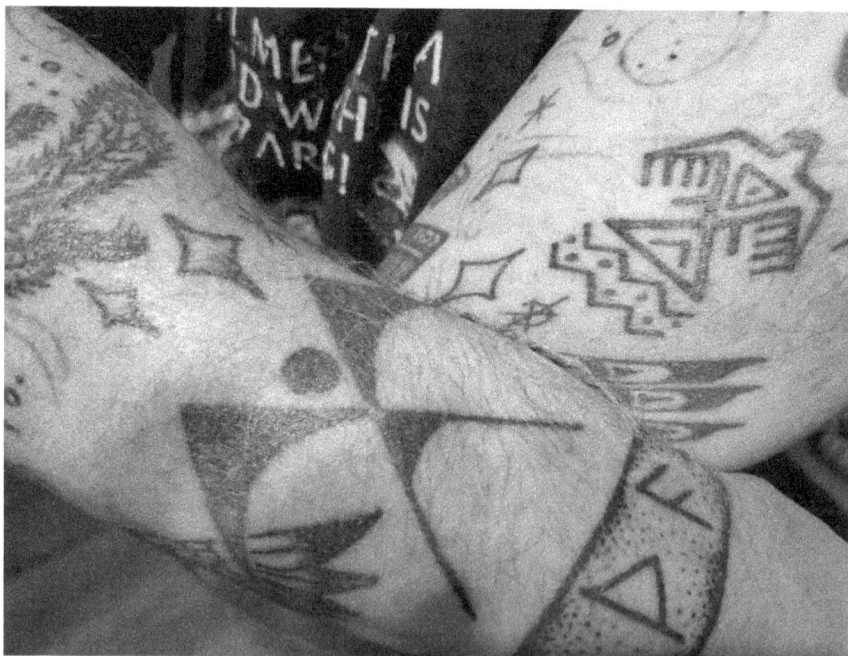

Coyote Chris:

After Mauna brushed me, I went out and got this done (points at Mauna Kea tattoo on right wrist), my buddy Jeremy Baker did that for me. And I have this (points to tattoo on left bicep) right here for the Standing Rock protectors that were trying to stop a pipeline going through their land. My one-time apprentice Autumn had texted me the day before Thanksgiving a few years ago and told me that a tattoo artist named Aaron Wall in St. Louis was doing a design that showed a Thunderbird protecting the water for $50 and that all the proceeds were going to Standing Rock. It was a one-day offer, on Thanksgiving. I was having dinner out with my family and told them what Autumn told me and I asked who was in: Max was, and we booked an appointment for Thanksgiving Day.

Dave:

In my opinion, that makes the experience much more spiritual. Thanksgiving means something totally different to First Nation people. I think that is one of the more important messages you carry to people. Even though you are here in Southern Illinois, you have an awareness of, and sensitivity to, what is happening in the larger world around us. Do you see a sort of renaissance occurring globally where people are becoming more aware their spirituality? More aware of what the mountains or waters might have to say about mankind's impact on Mother Earth?

Coyote Chris:

On some days I get so hopeful. You see young Greta Thunburg who starts a year ago sitting outside the Swedish parliament with a sign saying, "School Strike for the Climate," and she goes from there to where she's talking to millions of people and then millions of children are walking out of school because they're concerned about the environment. In my practice, the Mother is everything. She is everything to us. She keeps us alive and we've been too damn reckless for too long. And I know this is probably a political, but I don't care. But you know, how else would you expect me to be? I love the land. I love the water. I love the air. More so because

I can touch it in different ways that other people mostly can't or won't.

But mostly because they won't. Anybody can touch this stuff the way I do, if they want to. It's not political, it's very spiritual and that's part of my job, you know. I didn't get into this because I watched *Dances with Wolves* or *Thunderheart* and decided I wanted to be a medicine person. I had a profound experience with Spirit and so when you say yes to that sort of thing you take on a responsibility become a protector yourself and you help people who are protecting the Mother. I wish I could have gone to Standing Rock, but it happened before I had both of my hips replaced and I was in no shape to go there.

Dave:

I know the time before your surgeries was hard, because you are so active and enjoy spreading your message to many people. It isn't an overstatement to suggest that being a shaman is a 24/7 pursuit for you and aspects of your spiritual path have crept into every aspect of your life. I don't think you'd have it any other way because it enables you to meet people, carry your message, and listen and learn from them. Just the other day you were in Iowa. You've got an event at Ashmore Estates coming up. How many events a year are you involved with?

Coyote Chris:

It depends anywhere from, counting the ones we do here, 15 or so and that's because I still work full time as you know and I have budget constraints and things like that. I would travel more if I could, but no trip is wasted. I mean you've heard me; I get up and give a talk about shamanism. I talk about shamanism or about ghost hunting, but there's always a message. You have to listen to the message, too. I put it in there subtly, but it's that we all have a gift and that gift is our will, our medicine gift from Spirit and then we have intent and that's what we do with our gift. Everybody has a gift inside of them; no one is excluded. I see so many people walking around numb, you know, that the Pink Floyd song "Comfortably Numb" starts playing in my mind.

So often I just wish for one second that they could feel what I feel sometimes. And sometimes, I'm not going to lie to you, sometimes having a gift sucks. It's a blessing and a curse. It is because last night I was like, very on guard because I've kept hearing booms around the house. Now I'm sure there's some rational explanation for it, but I have to think about other things too. Was it something that the Mother's trying to say, or was some elemental being voicing its displeasure? I have to consider these possibilities. My wife Julia says I'm kind of amped up too much sometimes, but you know, it's kind of way it goes. I have to shut it down a little bit at work while I do my normal job, but not so much that I lose my awareness or my gifts.

I have a little statue of a coyote on my desk at work, so I don't forget too much, as sometimes you do forget because this is so hard. Anybody's who a practitioner that works a regular nine to five is immersed in our western culture and that is not very conducive to a spiritual path that was originally rooted in a tribal culture. The First Americans with their tribal structures and their clans were always immersed in their spiritual path. We are not, as too many of us just worship on Sunday and pay lip service to our religion during the other six days. I see so many people that just have so much promise and you tell them that they have this light inside them, and they need to wake up. But, unless the right person finds them, or they have a spiritual experience that I had, they won't wake up. They can't because our culture is based on not waking up, it's based on staying asleep as you trudge along.

Dave:

That is a thing now. People talk about being woke. "Is that person woke?" is something we hear a lot in the metaphysical business. Woke has evolved into a verb to describe a consciousness state. But maintaining a balance between the day-to-day and being woke can be challenging. I don't know how you can shut it off and on. How do you maintain this balance?

Coyote Chris:

Well, I've been kind of blessed in the fact that I can shut it down a little bit. I know people who can't and it's a struggle for them to live a normal life. I know when to raise it up and when it's OK to bring it back down. So, I mean, when I go to an event, I will spend a lot of time working with people and doing things like that, but not always in the heightened state of awareness, but focused. But when a strong energy comes along, whether it's a wonderful person who I've got to talk to because they need to hear something, or somebody I know has a teaching for me and even to somebody who is a potential threat as well. So, I keep my awareness and energy on an even keel, normal kind of, and then it's like I've got like trip wires, I guess, that sets my alarm off and I'm ready to go in a heartbeat.

Dave:

Let's set all the paranormal stuff aside for a bit and talk about mediumship, psychic work or intuitive abilities. All these words can be used interchangeably, and I really believe they are different modalities for accomplishing the same thing. Tell me about the people you have worked with from a medium or psychic perspective – what sticks out in your mind the most? What is the common thread that brought people to you?

Coyote Chris:

That you get this feeling about a person, you know, or they come to see you and they don't know why they came to see you, saying they don't know why they're here. Or they just want to get their fortune told, now you know me, I don't tell fortunes. I give people spiritual readings, but they sit down with me anyway. Then after the reading starts all of a sudden you see that light come on and they're like, "You mean?" – "Yes, you have these abilities." And then you can kind of see them have that "aha" moment. Now, this awareness, this "aha" comes and goes. Because I remember when I woke up the first time it took me awhile. You have your ups and downs where you think this is fun and then you think it's bullshit. You run the whole gamut of emotions because it's so hard to believe, because we're not taught to believe these things but watching the eyes of someone who's "got it is so gratifying." Then they'll start telling you stories about themselves, about how they were in this situation and how they felt this, and then this happened. Things they have experienced and could not explain. They just need some kind of affirmation from someone they believe in to tell them, that yes, this is you. This is actually, truly you.

Dave:

Thinking back to the moment of your spiritual catalyst – the warrior dance at the pow-wow – do you think you had the that same look in your eyes as those who come to see you? What do you think your expression was when it hit you?

Coyote Chris:

I wish I had a picture of that.

Dave:

I would love to have been a fly on the wall

Coyote Chris:

I just I can't imagine what my face looked like as a agnostic nonbeliever went to, "Oh shit. There's something here. I don't know how to deal with it."

Dave:

So, the transformation was a less of a journey and more of an awakening? Like a brilliant flash within your subconscious? An immediate awareness of your calling? I cannot imagine what it must have felt like to have all these messages firing at you, especially since you had not learned to speak the "psychic" or "medium" language yet.

Coyote Chris:

And it had been firing before that. I thought I was going to this powwow, where I had this epiphany, for something social to do. Julia said, "Let's go to the powwow," and me, not knowing what it really was, what I was walking into, you know like we talked about last time. And this needed to happen because I was horribly depressed. I was seeing and feeling things from other people and didn't know why. I worked with delinquent adolescents back then who were damaged, very damaged and feeling and seeing what they were feeling and seeing, and I didn't know how to deal with it. So, it's like Spirit says, "Okay, we better push this guy harder." Because looking back I can see where they had tried before, but I was too dense to pick it up. But yeah, it's been wild.

Dave,

In your career, you work with a broad array of people. You have to be high-functioning and very clever to manage your caseload of work. But that high-functioning perspective is really very mechanical. Take all the non-mechanical stuff you learned along your path and layer it over the day-to-day stuff. Which one do you go to more often – mechanical or intuitive? The day-job skills or the more comprehensive understanding of the world you developed as a shaman?

Coyote Chris:

That is still my guiding principle this day. I use the shamanic stuff to augment, to explain what I feel and see. And so, I've been in this business of social services a long time, so now what I do is like, okay, this is what I feel now, and then I back it up with observational data. And so, I write reports that go to the state office and to other places of importance, like funding sources and you can't be putting down that a spirit told you something, or you divined something.

Dave:

If you did do that, I suspect someone would be knocking on your door.

Coyote Chris:

They would, they'd be after me and we wouldn't be sitting here talking today.

Dave:

You have developed some notoriety in Alton, Godfrey and the Riverbend area of Southern Illinois. Correct me if I'm wrong on this, but haven't you assisted law enforcement with solving some cases?

Coyote Chris:

Yeah. I mean, it's been more peripherally. I was asked by the Indiana State Police one time to get in a small plane to look for guy. But the whole thing was kind of curious. One, I wasn't getting into a little two seat airplane. I'm wasn't going to do it. At least at that time, I might do it now. But I truly felt that this guy didn't want to be found pretty quickly into my investigation and I told the police this. He hadn't come home and later they discovered his truck at work with the keys and his wallet with $400 in it. Poof, he was gone leaving behind his wife and kids who understandably were devastated. When I initially spoke to his wife, I knew there was something up, you know, that this guy wasn't killed, this guy wasn't abducted or anything like that. A psychic was on the case as well and we both saw him in a truck heading to Chicago after I had a vision of him hiding in a cabin in Indiana. That was what brought me to the attention of the Indiana State Police. After talking to his wife some more I found out that his upbringing would lead to something like this, that he would just disappear. He had been adopted when he was in elementary school and basically his adoptive parents changed his last and first names and it seems they tried to make him forget his past and mold him into their own image. Without a true sense of self, it wasn't surprising that couldn't take the pressure of being a father and husband and he split.

Dave:

How has this impacted your relationships with friends and family? There must be some positive and negative impacts on individuals who experience similar journeys. What were the impacts on your spouse, your children and your community?

Coyote Chris:

And that's a problem a lot of people have, and that is quite true. That's a good question. Initially all this did not go well with my wife. Julia was not overly pleased and looking at it from the outside in I understand that. The man she married had flipped and gone off in a totally different direction. Then early on I was off meeting with teachers like Jim Gillihan and Johnny Moses and after that came the spiritual and paranormal events which led to appearances on TV shows. So as time went on, I was away on weekends more and more and away from her and Emily and Max. Now when I was really travelling a lot the kids were older and doing their own things anyway. However, sometimes they would come with me on some of my trips. Emily went with me when I presented at my first big convention, The Scarefest in 2013, and Max went with me to The Scarefest the next year and has done other conventions and public events with me. Julia, who thought that conventions would be boring, finally joined me at The Scarefest in 2018 and had a great time. All three have done paranormal investigations with me and we actually did a Sutton Family paranormal investigation event at the Mineral Springs in 2019 and had a blast together. Julia met Dustin Pari (*Ghost Hunters/ Ghost Hunters International*) and thinks so much of him that she bakes a pie for him every time one of us is going to see him, Elizabeth Saint (*Ghosts of Shepherdstown*), who has always been good to us, came over to Emily's and her husband Tyler's house for drinks the weekend of an event, we had a family dinner with Robb Demerest (*Ghost Hunters International*), which included you and Donna, and Julia and I talked with John Zaffis over breakfast about how he he sent Brian Cano into the darkest, nastiest places on *Haunted Collector*. Dan Klaes, who owns the Hinsdale House, is a family friend as is Wes Forsythe (Scarefest Television and who booked me on my first podcast), and his wife Anita. Plus, all of them have been in circle with Johnny Moses. So, I guess that the best way to deal with notoriety is to stay humble and let your family into your other world so then can enjoy it with you.

Now, like I've said before Julia was none too keen about my shift into the mystic and at one time, she was ready to give me the "what for" about it. Again, this was back in the late nineties. and I really love telling this story as it shows how Spirit works sometimes. So, she was sitting at the kitchen table going over this in her mind about how she's going to bring this to my attention, when a rock I had picked up from a nearby creek that was on the table on front of her started rolling. Now this could be attributed to an uneven table or some type of vibration. However, as Julia told me, the rock that rolled had only three sides. The round ones stayed put.

So, at that point she decided that it would be best to let this play out. Now she has been the person in my life who has tried to get my head out of the clouds and has tried to calm me down and bring me back down to earth. Sometimes it's aggravating, but I understand it. So, she helps ground me, even if sometimes she's wrong [laughs], but it does help me overall.

Dave:

I have grown close to your family over the years I have known you and your children are incredible – they definitely talk the talk, but they are probably not yet ready to walk the walk. Fair to say they crawl the walk. But Max, your son, shares much of the knowledge, skills, and abilities you possess.

Coyote Chris:

He does, and he's also been exposed to the paranormal work more as he tends to enjoy that part. It's like Max got the ability to sense and use energy while investigating and Emily received the psychic gifts. Max loves the hunt in the dark, which I love too, you know, because he's a big strong guy and he's into walking around in dark, nasty places with me looking for creepy things. Emily, on the other hand, she's very sensitive and empathic and is very good at reading people and perceiving spirits. I think she's probably got more psychic talent than she's letting on and she could do healing work as well. Emily does do paranormal investigations, but Max doesn't show much interest in the psychic and healing even though he does have skills in those areas. But it's tough when you're a young adult to spend much time on this type of work. Both are establishing their homes, families, and careers, which is now eating up a lot of their time, as well as trying to find time to do things with their friends.

I mean, when you're trying to walk your spiritual path and start coming into your medicine when you're a young adult, as it's hard because you've got children, you've got a partner, and other responsibilities. I've talked to so many young people about this and it's like, "I don't have the time and I need to put this on the back burner." And yeah, I get that. I've worked with one student, whose name is Autumn, on and off for the past 20 years. She started working with the shamanic teachings that I do share, actually she's the closest thing I've ever had to an apprentice, but she got married, had a kid and I didn't hear much from her for a while. She would let me know how things were going and talk about some spiritual stuff once in a while, but that was it for a few years. She pops back around more frequently now, and we talk about teachings and other ways of using her gifts. She has studied other traditions and has forged her own kind of eclectic practice that works well for her and I think that is really cool. She did what she needed to do and came back to improve herself even more.

I've had to do it and other people have had to do it. The thing is you can't give up. You have to do what you can do when you can. You just can't say, "Well, God gave me these gifts and I'm going to do this and I don't give a shit what my family thinks about me not being around while I chase after my spiritual power." Well, that doesn't play well with your family, first off. Second, it's not going to play well with Spirit either because you're given these gifts for a reason, but not at the expense of your family life and taking care of your children and being a good husband or wife or partner. So, sometimes you have to put yourself on hold and take care of your responsibilities. It's OK. Spirit understands and will wait patiently until you are free to do more of your work.

Dave:

Let's focus on your path. What were the first steps on your path?

Coyote Chris:

First thing I ever did was reading Tarot cards. Now as I shared before I was taught how to read Tarot by Gunn Hollingsworth, which was good as I was so new to doing psychic work that I

75

needed someone to teach me. He taught me using the Native American Tarot deck, which I still use to this day, and showed me what the cards meant, how they related to each other, and even how you could use numerology with the card numbers as part of the reading. Now he only taught me this one spread, the way the cards are laid out, he called it the Tarot Mandala.

It's a pretty big spread, 21 cards in three rows of seven laid out so that there is a top. a middle, and a bottom row. The top row is past, the middle is present, and the bottom row is the future. So, I practiced a lot to get the know the cards until I felt I was ready. At the time I started reading cards we lived in the Kankakee, Illinois area and we had some friends who owned a coffee shop there and they agreed to let me do readings for their customers. I'll never forget the night of my first gig. I charged like five bucks a reading, something like that and I think I made about 15, 20 bucks and it went pretty well. I mean, most of my customers seemed pleased with what I told them, and nobody called me a fake or anything like that. So, it was all good. And so, I get me a little money and I'm a professional now, just feeling all crazy and good about myself. Then when I get home, there's a big pile of dirty dishes in the sink and it was my night to do them. And so, the "professional" had to go do the dishes.

Dave:
Life goes on, right?

Coyote Chris:
There is a saying that I read in a Buddhist text, "Before I was enlightened, I chopped wood and carried water. And then after I was enlightened, I chopped wood and carried water." You have to learn to be who you are and still take care of your responsibilities.

Dave:

And I have had to count on you to cover my responsibilities too! Not all that long ago I was out of town and realized I was booked to read Tarot on a river cruise in Grafton. I was 12 hours from Illinois, so I called Chris the day before I was scheduled to read and asked if he would cover the event for me.

Coyote Chris:

Actually, it was 12:20 at night.

Dave:

Well, it was 11:20 where I was so it wasn't that bad (laughing), but you handled it like a champ. All the lessons you learned in Chicago, all that knowledge about the Tarot, had fused both intuitive and instinctual for you. And I think that is what makes you special you don't even need cards to read people.

Coyote Chris:

Tarot cards are good for telling a story and you know, you're a Tarot reader, you're a good Tarot reader, but that's what the cards are good for. Without the cards you can pick up pieces of what you need to know and probably put together a reading, but with those cards out there you can you can just tell a story by interpreting the cards as you go through the reading. And people are like, "Oh yeah, yeah, yeah, yeah," and they, they relate to that. People need something to see whether you're doing Tarot or psychic work, healing work, paranormal work, so you need tools of some kind. People want to see flashing lights on meters during a paranormal investigation, people want to see rattles and smoke when you're doing healing work and it's the same doing psychic work. People, in my experience, like to have you be able to put something in front of them, whether it's Tarot, a numerology charts or runes or things like that. So, you can point to them, it makes it more of a real thing to them.

Dave:

I think as people begin to move down their path, they become more accepting of things which may explain the unexplainable in their lives. Whenever we conduct a paranormal investigation, folks always want to work with the Ovilus – the electronic device which produces words based on ambient energy in the environment. And there are always a lot of assumptions made about these words. People begin to say, "Oh, well, that's a story. Those are sentences. Let's throw a couple of verbs in there and we've figured it all out." But, as anyone who investigates knows, the most useful tool is this [Dave points to his heart] and that's all you really need. So, you started off with Tarot, which does have a lot of mechanical aspects – arcana, colors, numerology to name a few – but then you expanded in less mechanical ways. You began using your heart. Tell me about that.

Coyote Chris:

But then it's just, you know, and I still, to this day use the numbers, I use the suits, and the picture on each card. You start looking at them, and all of a sudden, they'll start talking to you.

Dave:

But what really changed:

Coyote Chris:

You said that I used to focus on the cards and that's true. Now It's like I use the cards to support what I'm feeling from this person. The cards fall in a way that if I feel that there's a father issue in their past, bam, right there on the row that shows the past there is a card that points to a negative male presence. Then it comes to me in greater detail what that issue was, so I use my medicine to expand the cards are showing. The cards and I work together in synchronicity, so again it's just a tool to help tell a story and the cards that need to come up do.

Dave:

What you accomplish with folks now is much more comprehensive. You are talking about root causes of things which go back years, decades, maybe even generations in families.

Coyote Chris:

That's as it should be, because when I do a reading it's about looking into a person and not only seeing what causes their anxiety is, what is causing their other issues of today, and to be able to talk to them about it. I've been talking with people about their issues for 30 freaking years in my day job in social services and that serves me well here. But it's that this is not just a, "Here's what I see and here's what I feel." It's more like here's what I know you feel and here's what I see in you. This potential, right? And this is my secret. Okay. I'm going to tell you that my secret is that every reading, every time I meet with somebody, I want to pull out that potential, that they don't see, out to where they can see it and where they can believe it.

Because before, everybody's already told them that it's crap. I get so many people who have been raised in a way where they are told they are nothing, or that their budding mystical abilities are rubbish, if not evil, and to be "normal" like everyone else. But to be able to pull out this potential in them and to show them how they can succeed by bringing it out, how it can work for them, what the pratfalls will be. I tell them what's going to trip them up, because I know what is going to trip them up from our session and I tell them what to watch out for. I also talk with them about outside resistance, like a spouse or friends, who expect you to stay who you are and not change and how to deal with that.

Dave:

What about you personally? When people come to you and they're seeking answers and they've exhausted all the non-esoteric ways of figuring things out – they have been to see a medical doctor, sat with a psychiatrist, attended church, school, or support groups – but now they are coming to Coyote Chris Sutton. That means they are embracing your role as a shaman, psychic, healer, empath and medium. And they find answers to their unexplainable challenges or dilemmas. But, what about you? What are your vulnerabilities? What keeps you up at night? What's the one thing, if you had to pick anything, that remains unanswerable for you?

Coyote Chris:

What scares me? It's very hard to describe, but it's like mortality in and of itself does not scare me. How I come to my physical life's end scares me. My father died of Alzheimer's and the last way I want to go out is this way. Seeing my father who was a brilliant, brilliant man wither away mentally was horrifying to me. We started to realize that something was off when one day when we were playing Trivial Pursuit and he lands on Arts and Entertainment, you know, books and stuff like that. And the question was, "Who was Tiny Tim's father in *A Christmas Carol*?" Now, my father taught *A Christmas Carol* in his English classes for years and could throw quotes from the book all day long. But on this day, he did not know the name of Tiny Tim's father, Bob Cratchit.

Dave:

How did that affect your father?

Coyote Chris:

Scared him. He played it off because that's how my dad was.

Dave:

How did it affect you?

Coyote Chris:

Scared me. Yeah, I thought, "Here we go." You know that's the start of "the long goodbye," that's what Alzheimer's is. He lived another 10 years and died at 91 not knowing who he was.

Dave:

I've never asked you about that before. I was not expecting something nearly so personal. So that takes a second to digest.

Coyote Chris:

I don't mind being honest about that. I actually talked to Julia the other day about how I'm starting a different diet that improves your mind function. Now my father's father did not have Alzheimer's. My maternal grandfather died of a stroke. I've got that under control, you know, I take meds to help with that.

Coyote Chris:

And your mother passed away not too long ago. It's been about a year or two.

Coyote Chris:

Yeah, she had congestive heart failure, that and kidney issues. That's all on her side of the family and her sisters all had the same thing. They all lived to be in their late eighties. Yeah, but she had it together cognitively until the very end.

Dave:

So, for you, it is the fear of losing cognitive function and awareness?

Coyote Chris:

Yes, and I believe that after I give up the mortal coil that I'm back there and aware again, but that interim time scares the shit out of me. And you know, there's other things that scare me, but nothing like that. You and I have walked in the darkest places and just swagger in there. That stuff doesn't scare me, that stuff never scares me.

Dave:

And you know ghosts aren't going to do anything to us.

Coyote Chris:

No, I know... Well, they might, but I'm not scared anyway. If I was going to go out, I'd rather go out like Gandalf on the bridge of Khazad-dum in The Lord of the Rings and die that way than be 91 and in hell. I think that it would an honor if I could die in the service of somebody, just like the same oath you took when you were in the Navy for 30 years. I would rather do that than to die like my father had to.

Dave:

It is more meaningful in many ways. I speak on occasion about the concept of Three Deaths as embraced by Buddhists. It is that third death that really, truly matters. As long as there is a recollection of someone, as long as they're still alive in your mind, then they're not dead because you're still recalling them. The key to avoid Third Death is to pass memories along on to future generations, so the person lives in perpetuity. They don't ever go anywhere. They're always with us.

Coyote Chris:

Oh yeah, and in other ways too. After he had died, I saw my dad one time when Max and I were out playing tennis. Between a volley I glanced up at my car and he was sitting there watching us. Yeah. He loved tennis and coached the tennis team where he taught school for several years and I'm sure he was proud to see his grandson playing as well.

Dave.

And I know he lives in your heart because I hear you drop pretty spot-on literature references, so his influence remains in your life. To me, that is a really beautiful thing to have. Talk to me about when you became known locally as Coyote Chris Sutton. When did the calls start coming in to help with spiritual house cleansings and helping people?

Coyote Chris:

So, I was kind of coming at it in a roundabout way because I kind of set up shop out in Bethalto at Little Shoppe of Auras, Sandy's place. So, I was doing that stuff, but again, on the down low, and most of the people asking for asking for house cleansings were not going to know the people who I associated with in the Alton High Booster Club that I was a member of to help raise money for the kids' sports teams. But there's never been a mad rush. I've always been doing a lot of different spiritual and mystical things and the gigs come and go in spurts I've noticed. Because I do so many different things that it's never, like I'm terribly bogged down with house cleansings and things like that. It seems like I get the call when I'm needed, and my skills fit the situation well. But there are also times, even a couple with you, where I've been on cases where it's like, it's total BS. You go to houses where there are other issues and it's not about ghosts and demons from the pits. It's about the much more common demons in these homes which, sadly, are drugs, alcohol, violence and mental health issues. The people involved in these situations call people like us because they are sure that something evil is causing their problems. You try to help them see the real issues, but it's too often fruitless. You leave and they just call someone else till they hear what they want. (Note: some ghosts may come around for the negative energy flying around, but they are not the cause in these situations) And I know a lot of people and paranormal teams who won't do house calls anymore because of this.

Dave:

Absolutely. Donna, my wife, and I are reluctant to go on house calls. I've seen a disproportionate amount of addictions and addictive behaviors in homes – those addictions were the "haunting" in the home, not anything spiritual.

Coyote Chris:

Because people want to externalize it. I mean, they don't want be seen as being a drug addict or an alcoholic or as a violent cad. They want to make it about demons doing all these things to destroy them and hurt their family and things like that, because people don't want to take responsibility for their lives and actions. It's one of the most difficult things a person has to do, and this is one thing you really have to do walking this path. You've got to know who you are and you damn well got to be real honest with yourself.

Dave:

That was my next question. How do you see yourself when you get up in the morning? Are you Chris Sutton, husband, Chris Sutton, father, Chris Sutton, community member, or Coyote Chris Sutton, shaman?

Coyote Chris:

It is all one, because that's all me.

Dave:

But is it a lot to have to manage?

Coyote Chris:

Not if one just manages it as it comes. Yeah. It's when you start thinking about having to do all this, and this, and this, and this so much that you overwhelm yourself. Everybody's got to do this day-to-day stuff and so on to varying different degrees. I practice shamanism and I go do readings, stuff like that. Some people are Shriners and they're into clubs and things like that.

Dave:

True, but they can take off their Shriner's hat, you can't exactly hang the shaman moniker at the door. You've made the choice, the conscious choice, to be who you are and what you are. So, you walk in a place and people say, "Who's this guy? Holy cow, there's something different about him."

Coyote Chris:

I don't like that.

Dave:

Well, they do. I see it and hear it all the time.

Coyote Chris:

I think the thing that shines through is the base for what I do. Everything in my life is through my spiritual connection. That connection with Spirit, with the land, with Gaia, you know, Mother Earth, the sky, that's what shines. This just augments everything else. It heightens everything else. What did you do in the community, what you do as a father and a husband, it makes it better? If you're being honest with yourself and you're following through on being the best person you can be it just makes it better.

Dave:

We have talked about where you've been, but where do you think Gaia will take you next?

Coyote Chris:

I try to guess. It's not a good guess.

Dave:

Where do you want it to go?

Coyote Chris:

I don't know. I am content. I mean, it sounds odd, you know, as most people have goals and things like that. This is one thing I am working on, I want to do bigger paranormal and spiritual conventions, mostly because I want to be around more people. So, if I give a presentation hopefully more people will be there. And that's not because I want to be a TV star or something like that, because I know if I start thinking that way, things will go off the rails real fast, I just have to accept it. I accept my medicine, which is to help other people become woke, to find themselves, to find themselves spiritually, and bringing light to the darkest places.

That's what I do. It doesn't matter whether it's a paranormal event, a psychic fair, if I'm doing healing work. It doesn't matter. That's the overlying principle. That's what I'm here to do. I'm not here to be a great teacher. I do teach people, but if you notice, I don't teach constantly. I do a few classes every year at the Mineral Springs and I enjoy it. But you know, people have asked me to be like a mentor and things like that, I don't mind communicating with and helping people, but I just don't want to take people under my wing.

Dave:

Your strength is working one on one with people. There's not a doubt in my mind because I've seen you do. And, one of the things that I think, and this is not meant to be sort of the mutual admiration society here, but I think one of the things that's most important about what you do is you approach each person without any preconceived ideas or solutions. You look at people as individuals and you also do not see them for the demographics that society puts around them. Race, color, creed, orientation, income, doesn't really matter. None of that stuff is important. You look at the soul, that astral plane existence that someone has in this physical plane and connect with them and give them insight into things that they might not otherwise see. So, when you talk about bringing the light to the darkest places, sometimes the darkest places we could ever have as a one-on-one relationship with somebody, I mean, I know I've seen it.

Some of the things that we get to deal with in this line of work, when we bring someone to us or someone comes to find us. It can just be off the charts dark, and you come to a place like Mineral Springs like this, and, you know, it's haunted. I got all of that, but it's not dark. And there's nothing that we do during an investigation in a place like this that's significantly that much different every time. I mean, it, it is what it is. The building's pretty consistent. But man, when those people come in, though, we can have that one person though, that comes from an investigation that is super dark, super strong, negative energy, and you latch onto that. I've seen you do it every single time where you recognize it. And I'll even see you focus more on that one person kind of put your arm around them, not metaphorically your arm, around them as you lead them around and talk about the experiences that they're having. And you draw this negative strain of energy out of them and mold it and work with it and then I see you throw it away. It's amazing.

Coyote Chris:

That's just what I do. It's innate. I just, you know, I don't even think about. I see this person and it's like, "I gotta talk to this person." I just know it and I follow through. They're here for a reason. And I've seen this too where somebody show up for an event and it's like, why the hell is this person here? All of a sudden you can brush those negative energy cobwebs that hide them away and you look at who they really are and think, "Oh, that's why they're here." Yeah, they need something from you to help them grow.

Dave:

This path you're on is not all that narrow. It is pretty wide, and I think you will always make room to allow others to walk alongside you. How do people find you?

Coyote Chris:

You know, that's a good question. I mean, obviously I have a website and I am on Facebook and all these other things. Some people find me that way. A lot of times they don't know how or why they find me; they just find me. And those are the ones that really need you, because Spirit brought them to you.

Dave:

Of all the different sort of modalities that Coyote Chris Sutton practices, one area we didn't really address is healing. Healing is something that most folks look at with a skeptical eye, mostly because they haven't experienced it or understand what is involved. Tell me about shamanic healing.

Coyote Chris:

Well, to me, and this is the way I've been taught and the way I've observed, is that it's not about me. My job is to cleanse myself enough to where Spirit, God or whatever you want to call it, chi maybe, comes through as uninhibited as it can. Because we all carry around stuff inside us that clogs us up, worries, fears, anger. When I'm preparing to do healing work, I do it the way I was taught. I learned that when you become a "hollow bone" you bring energy from earth and sky. While you're bringing these energies in, you will feel some of those negative feelings or negative energies inside you. When you do you pull them out with your hands and throw them up to Spirit. Then after you feel the energy flowing freely you focus on people, a loved one, somebody in your community and somebody in the world and send them healing energy, which allows the energy to flow out of you to those who need your medicine.

Energy flows the whole time when you're doing healing work and so by becoming a "hollow bone" you're telling your body that the energy will continue to flow, like water through a fire hose. So, then you're ready to go. You've become a "hollow bone" and now it's time for you to get to hell out of the way and let that connection with Spirit tell you what to do. Dave, you know, I carry around my backpack and I have everything I need in there to do healing, divination, and paranormal investigations. I've seen people carry steamer trunks full of stuff, basically that's what it looks like, but that's okay if that is how they walk. I have seen people who have a stone for everything from demonic possession to a skin rash. I carry quartz crystals and a few little stones and that covers it all. You can tell quartz crystals what to do and they'll provide what you need. They're like a spiritual Swiss Army knife, they do anything. I do like other stones as I'm fond of amethyst and selenite. I use different wands of selenite for healing and paranormal work and I also use a rattle and a feather and smudge when I do healing work. And as I've said before, a lot of people believe that these items are the "thing" itself and they're not the "thing" itself. They are only tools. They remind me to focus on what I'm doing, on my will and my intent. I've got the will, my medicine gift that flows through me and my intent is how I use it to help others. These tools that I use are helping me focus the energy to where I want it to go. So, I have all these things going and the energy flowing through me, but I have to remember that it's not mine. It's not mine, but I'm borrowing it, so to speak, or willing it to come through me and guiding it into people who need it. When I do healing work I move my hands through the energy that everyone has emanating from their body when I begin so I can feel where the problem areas in the body are. I rarely touch people. When I feel a place that has negative energy in it I send the healing energy to that spot. I even get a little jazzy sometimes and I use the chakras too, like your wife Donna does when she does Reiki. So, I go to the crown and the other chakras because it works. I can feel the energy there, so why not?

Dave:

There are so many different ways to describe the same thing, whether it's a Native American modality, a Dharmic modality, like chakras, or a Western philosophical modality. One of the most interesting things you have taught me is the "Hollow Bone" technique.

Coyote Chis:

I refer to it more as a meditation.

Dave:

Who taught the "Hollow Bone" meditation to you?

Coyote Chris:

That actually came from Frank Fools Crow and he taught it to a lot of people. He was a Lakota holy man that we've talked about before.

Dave:

Tell me about the first time you performed the "Hollow Bone" mediation. Do you remember the experience? Because I remember when you taught me and I remember exactly what happened.

Coyote Chris:

It's funny, I had actually learned it first before I met anyone who could teach it to me. I read a book about Fools Crow called *Fools Crow: Wisdom and Power* by Thomas Mails. The book is written in an interview format and in it Fools Crow describes it. So I did it from that. This was before I met Jim Gillihan and these other guys who knew Fools Crow. As far as the first time I did it is coming back to me now. It's it was, it was pretty cool. I mean, because back then it was like having sex for the first time. Your body has these really crazy feelings, you know? And so yeah. It's like that.

Dave:

Like astral travel?

Coyote Chris:

It is, it's just a rush and you feel so connected to Spirit. And even to this day, I still feel the same way when I do it. It's just hard to describe. For example, last week at Coyote Chris' Crazy Chaotic Spiritual Circle. we had "healing night" where we took turns doing healing work on each other. And so, we started it with all of us becoming hollow bones. I hadn't done it since I had my second hip replaced, so in the back of my mind, I was thinking, "Well, I hope this works. I hope the power goes up and down the titanium." Of course, it did. and it worked just fine. But yeah, it was one of those little silly things you think about. It's just it is like that, I mean, it's just that amazing. I wish I could teach exactly what the freaking connection is like. I wish I could show you these colors and energies come out of my hands and how they course through my body.

You know, I teach people sometimes and sometimes I like to take them out to the woods. There is a nice forest preserve here in Godfrey at The Nature Institute. One of the best ways to teach people how to experience energy of another being is to find a good-sized tree, as trees have the most wonderful energy and they will exchange it with you. You can get this flow going between you and that tree by projecting your energy into the tree and then the tree sends it's energy back. I used to take some of the kids I used to work with out to similar places and they were just amazed. These city kids were in an area with all these trees and I would have them do this and they could feel the trees. They were so amazed. Then I would tell them that they would never have to be alone again, that the trees were always there for them.

Dave:

And that brings us back to where we started when we were talking about this broader, grander awakening that is going around the world regarding environmentalism and social activism. I don't know how you would capture this, but as a shaman in a mostly secular world, do you sense people are becoming more aware? I read a New York Times article the other day which reported the tremendous shift of people who are embracing Neo-paganism, Wiccan, Norse shamanism – and all of these different spiritual traditions in the 21st century. Things are changing rapidly, and people appear to walking away from contemporary religious paths that have failed to explain to them how to address the spiritual feelings in their heart. What is your daily walk like?

Coyote Chris:

It's so strange because I feel that hope, I see these people who are concerned about the climate, who are championing the Mother and who are trying to connect with Spirit, or they're trying to connect with the Chi which is also part of the earth, but that is more Buddhism and Taoism, which is also amazing stuff. I really love Taoism. And here's a side note, really quick, study these Eastern spiritual traditions, because these Eastern traditions are pretty cool. And I read about all kinds of different religious and spiritual traditions so that if I come across someone from a different tradition from mine, I could speak their language. But yeah, there's all these people trying to do these different spiritual things and I've started to feel this hope welling up in the world.

But there's also this darkness and it's very, very scary right now as well. And I thought about this the other day and it's probably overreacting, but I got a sort of a feeling like it's almost like being in Stephen King's *The Stand*. Now we haven't had a plague that's wiped out 99% of population, but we have a group of people gathering in the darkness and you have people who people gathering in the light. So, is this going to balance out or what's going to happen? You know, usually when you've got this type of energy moving around, there's bound to be some type of reaction and one way or another. It's not going to remain static. So, I mean, there are these wonderful spiritual energies mixing with these dark energies of hate, so there will be some type of reaction to these forces slamming into one another.

Dave:

History has these periods of religious revivalism, and history has periods where we turn our backs towards what folks call the church. People look to alternative modalities for understanding the world that they live in… and the pendulum swings.

Coyote Chris:

Yes, it seems to go up and down. I mean, there were times in the late seventies, early eighties, and in the nineties, when there was a big interest in Native American spirituality and there's just not one Native American spiritual tradition of course, there's 500 something different ones, but that's what people were into. Now it seems like it's not so much. People are trying other things like Reiki, Core Shamanism, and the pagan traditions. Interest in different traditions comes in ebbs and flows. But it's all good. I mean, these other traditions all good as they are leading people to good places. And it doesn't matter to me, it's whatever works for each individual. I just happened to show up at a freaking pow-wow and that's why I'm where I'm at now. I mean, if I had gone to a Renaissance fair or a pagan picnic, I might've ended up differently. I might be wearing Viking horns and carrying an ax around or something like that. Who knows?

Dave:

The butterfly flapped its wings at a pow-wow decades ago and look at the trajectory that you have been on ever since.

Coyote Chris:

That's exactly right. This is how it is and that's where Spirit put me. That's how I truly believe. Now certain things had to happen in my life before I got to where I needed to be. I'd had a fiancé when I was in college and we broke up, I had a wife for 15 months and we divorced. Then I married Julia. If I don't marry

Julia, I don't go to the pow-wow because it was her idea. I tell people all this is her fault in jest, but things like that happen for a reason. That trajectory depends so much upon so many things. You look at your life and it reads like a novel and there's parts in novels where some bad stuff happens to the main character. No novel is any good without that and you have to look at your own life like it's a novel and you're the main character who went through all this bad stuff. and this bad stuff hurts. You hurt. I tell people this all the time to take heart because you went through this bad stuff, the pain, you had to go through mistreatment, whatever it was, a bad marriage, bad parents, whatever. And I tell people that they went through that so that they could survive their pain, heal themselves and then hold their hand out to another person who is experiencing the same type of pain and help them heal, survive, then help others.

Dave:

Life puts you where you're supposed to be and until you have that vacancy, that chasm, that place where energy needs to go, you can't receive it. To me, that is the most beautiful thing about you. The universe puts people in your path and as you walk your path, you encounter these folks. What an amazing path!

Coyote Chris:

I like to think so. Yeah, it's worked out so far.

Dave:

And, and it's just, "Hey brother, take a drink, have a bite. I can help you."

Coyote Chris:

Here's a match, let's light you up.

Dave:

That's what it's all about. What else should we talk about tonight?

Coyote Chris:

Ooh, let's see. God, I can always talk about anything. You talked earlier about where to go next and that's such an interesting question to me because I love to entertain it. Part of me would love to know, but I think that, and this goes for everybody, not just me that people get so far looking ahead that they miss what's right in front of them. I had to learn that. I always like to say that life is like a three-act play, but you always need to be in the second act. If I'm in the second act and I'm thinking about something I did wrong in the first act, I'll mess up in the second act. If I'm in the second act and I'm worried about a difficult line in the third act I'll mess up in the second act. The second act is the present, so stay there and leave the past and future be.

But, you can make plans. I make plans. What I mean by planning is that I have put myself in a place where I can go different places because of what I can do. I can talk about shamanism, I can talk about spirituality, I can talk about ghost hunting and I put my own personal experiences into them.

Dave:

Those plans are logistics. And those plans are mechanical. I'm going to go to this place and do this thing in this amount of time. What you're talking about is spiritual – where do we go from here? Where do you go from here? It's not logistics. This is the spiritual journey that you are on and where does it take you? It is simple – we got put in front of each other a few years back at exactly the right time the Universe needed to happen so that could forge this bond, this friendship.

Coyote Chris:

You thought I was coming in to rob the shop. [laughs]

Dave:

Well, yeah. I mean, that was the word on the street. But it was serendipity or kismet or whatever you want to call it. It doesn't matter to me; we were supposed to meet.

Coyote Chris:

And our families were supposed to meet.

Dave:

And that is exactly the strength you bring to the table as a shaman for the people who need to find you. Your ability to impact those around you. Not necessarily straighten or alter their trajectory in life, but to put your arm around them and show them that there is more to life. And their hat path is very broad and beautiful just like yours has been. That's what it's all about.

Coyote Chris:

It is. Thank you so much, Dave.

# Afterword

It has been over a year since the second video was filmed and things have certainly changed. There has been a tremor in the Force with the COVID-19 pandemic, natural disasters, and all the hate rhetoric that has poisoned civil discourse in our country, and many of us are feeling it. In times like these it is the strength that I receive when I allow Spirit to work through me that keeps me going. Early in the pandemic my fear of the virus and an issue at work lead me into an episode of anxiety that affected me greatly. However, anxiety and I are old enemies and I know how to beat it. With help from some wonderful people, the energy of Spirit, and my belief in myself I got up off the mat and I am doing great today. Just because you walk a spiritual path does not mean you stop being a human being, but it does help you avoid issues that trapped you in the past and you can rise up stronger and quicker after a fall.

Not everything has been gloomy, in fact there have been many joys as well. My daughter Emily was married to her husband Tyler in June of 2019, Max is in a relationship with a splendid lady and her adorable son, and Julia and I have been able to work throughout the pandemic from home and learned how to survive being home together all day for which we are grateful. In January of 2019, Dave, Donna and I all appeared on *Ghost Adventures*

("Curse of the Riverbend: The Mineral Springs") and it was great fun. I was on the road a lot in 2019 for conventions and events and was happy to see many old friends and make new ones. Also, in 2019 I had both of my arthritic hips replaced and I feel great and move so much better. If you saw me in person or watched any video of me over the last couple of years before the surgeries, you could tell I had a pretty bad limp. Now, from late 2019 to all of 2020 I have not been traveling much, but I have accomplished other things. At the end of 2019 a CD of Sis-Si Wiss medicine songs that I recorded came out, Emily and I with our friend Mike Waters did a music video as a tribute for Bud Summers, a late friend of ours, that Jordan videoed and edited; and I wrote this book. Having to change my life to protect my family, other people, and myself has been difficult at times, but instead of sitting around wanting something I could not have, I did things that I had never done before. It is not about what you cannot do, it is about what you can.

*Coyote Chris Sutton*
September 2020

# About The Author

Coyote Chris Sutton has been practicing shamanism for over 25 years and has been conducting paranormal investigations since 1998. He is a member of the Red Cedar Circle of Southwestern Illinois in the Si-Si Wiss medicine tradition of the Pacific Northwest Coast and has practiced in that tradition since 2000. Chris has appeared on the paranormal television shows *Ghost Adventures*, *Dead Files Revisited*, and *Ghost Lab*, and he has been a presenter at several events and conventions for both the paranormal and the spiritual. He also has a degree in Social Justice and has worked in the social service field for over 30 years.

Coyote Chris Sutton lives in Godfrey, Illinois, with his wife of 30 years, Julia and they have two grown children, Emily and Max. And we all hunt ghosts!

Other Haunted Road Media titles in which Coyote Chris Sutton appears:

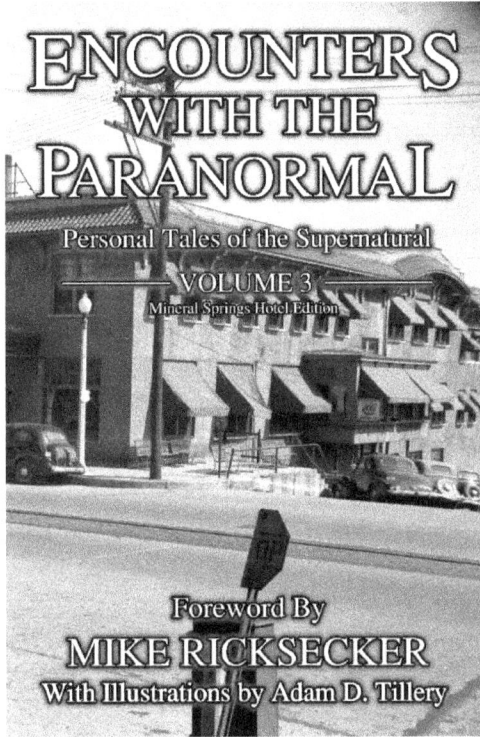

Almost everyone has a ghost story. Real people. Real stories.

In this third volume, read about more haunted houses, supernatural creatures, messages from pets from the other side, haunted history, experiences during paranormal investigations, psychic experiences, and more, including a dedicated section to the historic Mineral Springs Hotel. ENCOUNTERS WITH THE PARANORMAL: VOLUME 3 reveals more personal stories of the supernatural and paranormal, continuing to explore the realm beyond the veil through its contributors.

For more information visit:

# Haunted Road Media
www.hauntedroadmedia.com

www.ingramcontent.com/pod-product-compliance
Lightning Source LLC
Chambersburg PA
CBHW051734040426
42447CB00008B/1134